D1130126

HOLY GHOST FATHERS
FERNDALE
NORWALK, CONN.

HOLY GHOST FATHERS
FERNDALE
NORWALK, CONN.

SYMBOLISM and the CHRISTIAN IMAGINATION

SYMBOLISM and the CHRISTIAN IMAGINATION

HERBERT MUSURILLO, S.J.

HELICON PRESS
BALTIMORE DUBLIN

Helicon Press, Inc.
5517 Selma Avenue, Baltimore 27, Maryland

Helicon Ltd.
Dublin, Ireland

Library of Congress Catalog Card Number 62-13978

Nihil Obstat: EDWARD A. CERNY, S.S., S.T.D.
Censor Librorum

Imprimatur: ✠ LAWRENCE J. SHEHAN, D.D.
Archbishop of Baltimore
April 25, 1962

The *Nihil Obstat* and *Imprimatur* are official declarations that a book or pamphlet is free of doctrinal or moral error. No implication is contained therein that those who have granted the *Nihil Obstat* and *Imprimatur* agree with the opinions expressed.

To

VIOLA *and* STANLEY

who always encouraged me

to write this book

Printed in the United States of America
by Garamond Press, Baltimore, Maryland

Contents

Communication and the Christian Imagination

CHAPTER ONE

ALL THE religions in the history of the world have made use of symbolism; for every religious movement has attempted to express man's basic experience of the Holy, the Transcendent.[1] And for this task the ordinary dimensions of language and life have always been deemed inadequate. Through symbolism, however, words and things acquire a deeper and more subtle direction than they are normally called on to bear. Because of the openness of the symbol and its ability to relate quite disparate objects, man has been able to use symbolism to rise above the rim of the world like Plato and gaze, however briefly, upon the teeming heavens.

As far as Christianity is concerned, the first study of signs and symbols was made by Augustine in his book *On Christian Doctrine*.[2] Here Augustine stresses the importance of learning how to decipher the sign or symbol in order to comprehend the truth, whether it be the truth of the Scriptures or the truth of the physical universe. For Augustine, the way to the ultimate understanding of revelation lay through the forest of symbols which God had made in the world. Thus it is that man's basic medium of communication, the manipulation of the sensuous sound or

[1] See, for example, the classic treatment of Rudolf Otto, *The Idea of the Holy* (transl. from the 9th German ed. by J. W. Harvey), New York, 1923.

[2] *De doctrina christiana* I.2, II.1–3, and elsewhere.

sign, becomes the crucial element in the study of the Christian tradition.[3]

It is clear that the achievement of Christ has produced a distinct change in the relationships among men and, consequently, in their mode of communication. The earliest apostles were by the mandate of Jesus messengers or witnesses to announce the Good News (*evangelium*) to all men. Their message was, as we capture it in the first chapters of the *Acts of the Apostles*, the proclamation (*kerygma*) that the Messianic Atonement had been accomplished by the Servant of Iahweh according to Isaias the prophet. That Jesus had died, risen, and gone to his Father; and that all men should be baptized in his name and communicate in his mysteries until the end of the world. Thus, the primitive *kerygma* was a special sort of communication by those who had been witnesses of the redemptive mission of Jesus. It was not a coercion, but a simple, sincere message charged with the emotional conviction of those who had "seen, beheld, and handled concerning the Word of Life." This primitive *kerygma* and *didache* (the former to designate history and doctrine, the latter the moral implications for men) is the fountainhead of all theology and liturgy. Liturgy is the concrete cult expression of our adherence to the historic fact of Christ's Atonement; theology is man's attempt to discover the finite symbolic means of expressing the implications of God's intrusion in history. Theology will always entail tension, imperfection, and constant growth in man's struggle to bridge the gulf between revelation and language. It is the special use of linguistic symbols to explicate the primitive announcement of Good News. It is the reiteration of the Gospel by the Mystical Christ in the developing context of time and space.[4]

Thus the specifically Christian form of communication will, as I have suggested, necessarily be cast into a unique mould. All of man's psychic powers will be brought to collaborate in transmitting the Christian message in a manner that will be intelli-

[3] See Gerald Vann, *The Paradise Tree: On Living the Symbols of the Church* (New York, 1959).

[4] See H. Musurillo, "Symbolism and Kerygmatic Theology," *Thought* 36 (1961), 59–80, esp. pp. 73 *ff*.

gible to others. Thus arises the problem of the various forms or modes of expression: art, the liturgy, theology, philosophy. To those men who have come under the sway of the primitive Christian message there arises a new set of internal drives and propensities; the organism, with its storehouse of images, ideas, memories, etc., has been profoundly modified, but not completely changed. It is not to be expected that a man, when reacting to his environment in a Christian way, will be completely indistinguishable from all the rest.

In so far as symbolic communication is, in great part, the product of the projective or creative imagination encoding or transforming psychic experience, it follows that the imagination will always have a deep influence on any presentation of the Christian religious history. For the Fathers and early theologians the acceptance or rejection of the imagination was a crucial problem; and it is a dilemma that is still with us today. It is a problem that is not easy of solution, and one that will have wide repercussions throughout our theology and philosophy. But it may be said at the outset that there can be no question of acceptance or rejection: man's imaginative creativity cannot be long checked or suppressed; it is a human drive that must somehow emerge and have its way. We can do little more than plot its course and observe its function in all areas of human life. Man must be somehow accepted as he is. What is, however, a more fruitful question is: can we speak of a specifically Christian imagination, and, if so, what is its function? Is a Christian art possible, or should we rather speak of an art that happens to be practiced by Christians? To this question I believe a more positive answer can be given, based on what we know historic Christianity to be.

Even from the psychological point of view it would seem that there is, or at least should be, a specifically Christian imagination, one, that is, that has been elevated by Baptism into the Mystical Body, and has been impregnated by the truths, symbols, and liturgy of Revelation. However, the imagination of the artist or thinker need not always operate in a specifically Christian way; and thus it happens that what Christians produce in the area of art, or even philosophy, is often hardly distinguishable from the work of non-Christians. But the Christian imagination, when it is working in its specific function, is concerned precisely with the tension, the polarity, which arises between visible, sensuous reality and the hidden things which have been revealed to us, between the phenomena of time and the substance of things hoped for.

It took the early Christians some centuries to work out the possibilities of an art or a literature that could exist apart from catechesis and liturgy. Non-liturgical poetry, for example, had a most difficult existence. In the first place there was the problem of the adaptation of secular, pagan techniques to the needs of the growing Church. But why should the Christian write poetry at all when the means of salvation lay close at hand, in the Church and in the Scriptures? It was, I think, Paulinus of Nola who was the first to carve out a Christian theory of art and poetry. His famous tenth poem, written as an epistle to his former teacher Ausonius, puts the early Christian dilemma as well as it has ever been expressed. Ausonius, himself not too fervent a Christian, had urged Paulinus to resume his interest in poetry. And he replies:

> You urge me, Master, to take up again
> The Muses I have long abandoned. But why?
> Hearts pledged to Christ are closed to Apollo,
> And deny entrance to the goddesses of song.

And he continues:

> Another force, now, a greater God
> Urges me, demanding a new life,
> Claiming of us a sacred duty.

But it is clear that in the very writing of this new Christian verse he is settling the problem that vexes him. The very tension and conflict that he speaks of is precisely the stuff of Christian poetry; and as Paulinus says finally:

> Indeed, what the eye sees is but passing;
> Invisible are the things that are eternal,
> Glimpsed only in spirit and embraced by hope.

This then is the source of the authentic Christian artistic vision:

the tension between the supernatural and the tangible cosmos in which we are immersed. Sometimes there will be clash and seeming contradiction, when the brilliance of this world's light only heightens the shadow of faith, and all seems ambiguous and obscure. Yet at other times, the world of the Transcendent seems to complement the visible, and the universe is seen as a forest of symbols that can only be deciphered by the eye of faith. This is the dilemma, buried deep in the unconscious of the Christian, that is the wellspring of any specifically Christian art or literature. For as it is the role of Christian theology to express and develop in humanly intelligible symbols the message of Christian revelation, it is the province of art and literature not merely to repeat this message but rather to express the reaction of the Christian imagination to the newly awakened conflict of human existence.[5]

This then was the scope of early Christian art and poetry. But the artistic medium of Christian imaginative literature was slow in developing, growing as it did out of the Jewish Hellenistic world in which Christianity first found root. It is true to say that the symbolic technique of early Christian literature grew largely out of Judaism, and specifically from the sort of mystical interpretation of the Scriptures which we find in Philo of Alexandria, the Jewish scholar and philosopher of the first century of our era. Philo's pedantry combined in a peculiar fusion the urbanity of Hellenistic philosophy and the deep reverence for Moses and the prophets characteristic of the orthodox Hebrew teacher. And yet Philo's schooling in pagan philosophy and literature was no small element in his total approach; indeed, his technique is related to the Alexandrian and Stoic method of reading pagan literature on a moral-allegorical level for an edifying purpose. But, as applied to the Old Testament, Philo's methods are more closely allied with the practice of the rabbis and Jewish teachers, and with the private instruction handed down by secret groups of ascetics, of the sort we are familiar with since the discovery of the Dead Sea Scrolls community.

One of the most striking examples of the exegetical method may be observed in the Habacuc Commentary found at Qumran: here the words of Habacuc are applied to the Teacher of Righteous-

[5] H. Musurillo, *loc. cit.*, pp. 69 *f.*

ness. In Philo, we find an adaptation of the non-literal, or spiritual, interpretations of the Scriptures which were used by the Jewish teachers and are reflected in the *Midrashim.* For Philo, however, the spiritual interpretation is usually philosophical or ethical; and it is this secondary interpretation which Philo refers to as type, shadow, enigma, and mystery. For Philo, very often, the spiritual interpretation comes into play when the literal (or obvious) one offers difficulty; and many of the Alexandrian Fathers follow him even to the rejection of the literal sense on occasions when they found it "not suitable for God" (*ou theoprepes.*) This is the criterion of Alexandrian exegesis, and it extended even to the West in the commentaries of Ambrose, Augustine, and Jerome.[6]

[6] An understanding of the evolution of the fourfold sense is an essential key to the literature of this early period. For an important discussion of origins from the Philonic viewpoint, see H. A. Wolfson, *The Philosophy of the Church Fathers,* vol. 1 (Cambridge, Mass., 1956), pp. 24–72. Basic are Jean Daniélou, *Origène* (Paris, 1948), pp. 172 *ff.*, and his *Sacramentum Futuri* (Paris, 1950); *cf.* also C. Coppens, *Les harmonies des deux testaments* (Louvain, 1948); H. de Lubac, *Histoire et esprit: l'intelligence de l'Ecriture d'après Origène* (Paris, 1950); R. P. C. Hanson, *Origen's Doctrine of Tradition* (London, 1954); G. W. H. Lampe, and K. J. Woollcombe, *Essays in Typology* (Naperville, Ill., 1957), with the vast literature cited.

It is interesting to note the application, in the Middle Ages, of the fourfold sense to Dante's *Divina commedia,* which had wide applications elsewhere. The source for this was the famous Epistle 10, supposedly written by Dante to his benefactor Can Grande della Scala, to explain the meaning of the poem according to the categories of the Schoolmen. But the whole tone of the epistle hardly suggests a poet speaking of his own artistic creation and hence the letter may not be authentic: for the text, see E. Moore, *Le opere di Dante Alighieri* (rev. by Paget Toynbee, Oxford, 1924), pp. 414–420. For a discussion of the problem, see Dorothy Sayers, *Introductory Papers on Dante* (London, 1954), pp. 101–126. In any case, *Epist.* 10, § 6 distinguishes six elements in the discussion of any work: subject, form, author, purpose, title, and philosophy. In § 7 we are told that the *Commedia* is polysemous, having many senses; and an example is taken from the four senses of Scripture, messianic, moral, eschatological, and literal; in § 8, the author explains that the *Commedia* has two senses, the literal, which deals with "the state of souls after death," and the allegorical, dealing with "man insofar as by the use of his freedom in choosing good and evil he is liable to reward and punishment." Unfortunately, however, the epistle does not further explain how this is to be applied to the entire poem.

It was from Philo's sense of the "enigma" in Scripture that the Alexandrian catechetical school developed what we now call the allegorical sense. The typological interpretation is found in the Fathers of the second century, in Irenaeus, for example, and in Justin; but it was Clement of Alexandria and Origen who brought the method to a high degree of perfection. From the apologetic point of view, the leaders of the catechetical school realized that the Philonic technique was a flexible means of defending Christian doctrine and avoiding embarrassing difficulties. But Clement further saw the allegorical method as a way to explore the deeper meaning of the Scriptures, and to explain to the initiated Christian the *gnosis* or secret doctrine which could be handed on only by the approved teachers of orthodoxy. It is true, of course, that Clement's *gnosis* often results in trivialities, and the doctrines revealed by his spiritual exegesis are often eccentric and pedantic. Origen represents a clear advance over the primitive techniques of Clement. Apart from his distinction of the "somatic" and "pneumatic"—or bodily and spiritual—senses of Scripture, in which he closely approximates Philo, Origen (especially in his *De principiis)* presents a threefold structure which is highly illuminating. He distinguishes the flesh, the soul (*psyche*), and the spirit (*pneuma)* as the three components of the sacred Word; or, borrowing the Platonic terminology, Shadow, Image, and Reality. According to this threefold structure, the prescriptions of the Old Law were shadows, of which the true image is the Church of Christ; all will be fulfilled in the reality of the Last Day and the restoration of the world in heaven.

It was this Alexandrian-Origenist technique which ultimately developed into the so-called fourfold interpretation of Scripture: (1) the literal, or rather the obvious sense of the sacred text; (2) the messianic, in which Christ's redemptive work is suggested or foreshadowed; (3) the moral or tropological, in which some edifying moral doctrine is explained for the profit of the Christian soul; and, finally (4) the eschatological, in which are intimated the mysteries of Christ's Final Coming and the four Last Things. On the level of catechetical instruction, the Fathers under Alexandrian influence evolved a technique of Narration and Interpretation (*historia* and *theoria*), whereby the story of salvation from the beginning of the world would be interpreted in an allegorical way in order to fit in with the needs of the early catechumens. Indeed, all the different types of literary form used in the early Church—gospel, apocalypse, homily, treatise, edifying life, dialogue, and all the rest—are, in the last analysis, a unique fusion of Judaic and Greco-Roman elements which must be set against the scale of History and Symbol in order to understand the historical and dogmatic content.[7] In other words, the literary productions of early Christianity are symbolic forms of a peculiar type in which there is a subtle fusion of the doctrinal and the imaginative. Writers who, like St. John Chrysostom, came strongly under the influence of the Antiochene school, insisted more urgently on the liberal meaning of Scripture and tradition. Still, despite the opposition of the more literal school, the possibilities of allegory appealed to most patristic authors and made the scriptural commentary a most flexible and potent instrument in the evolution of Christian dogma. Indeed, as we shall see farther on, the Christian poets instinctively seized on allegorism as a rich source of poetic statement.

But in all the discussions of symbolic technique in the growth of Christian literature, we must not lose sight of the fact that the inspiration for the earliest Christian was always the liturgical acts which were the center of his new existence. The announcement of the Good News would terminate in the washing ritual of baptism, as we learn from the early chapters of the Acts of the Apostles. The preparatory prayers and readings from the Scriptures would culminate in the *agape,* or love-banquet, at the close of which the Eucharist would be celebrated. Thus the center of Christian life from the earliest days was the symbolic, ritual commemoration of Christ's achievement—for this is, indeed, the meaning of the liturgy. It is one vast, corporate symbolic gesture in which the enlightened participate in varying degrees. The washing by water is the entry-rite, the signal by which a man expressed his burial and resurrection with Jesus, and thus obtained the approval of the Christian community with the right to participate in their sacramental mysteries. The Mass, or the Liturgy *par excellence,* is indeed the archetypal sacrament, the focal, symbolic

[7] See H. Musurillo, "History and Symbol: A Study of Form in Early Christian Literature," *Theological Studies* 18 (1957), 357–86.

act of incorporation into Christ and the Church. For it may be said that all the other sacramental rites cluster around this central mystery as gestures of special sacred significance for all those who have been sealed with the Blood of the Lamb and await in vigilance the final coming of the Savior.

Thus all sacramental causality is heavily symbolic in so far as it derives from the redemptive act of Jesus and the significance He wished to be attached to it. As St. Paul and the Fathers constantly repeat, the Cross was the historic expression of man's reconciliation with God: the enmity is at last slain in the flesh. It is also God's definitive answer to the question raised by the suffering Job. For man now does not merely aquiesce to pain as part of the mystery of the cosmos; pain now becomes, by the act of Jesus, the means of man's own redemption. For the suffering of the second Job is an act of vicarious satisfaction and sacrifice, and an effective cause of the Atonement in the spirit of the second Servant song of Deutero-Isaias (chap. 53), the song that the Apostles and early Fathers so often referred to:

Yea, he hath borne our griefs
And carried our sorrows;
Yet did we esteem him stricken,
Smitten of God and afflicted.
For our sins was he wounded,
And bruised for our iniquities.
On him was the chastisement of our peace.
And in his stripes we are healed.
All we like sheep have gone astray;
Each has turned to his own way.
But Iahweh has laid on him the iniquity of us all.

Here we see the central image of the scapegoat applied to the Messiah of Israel. The lamb-symbolism emerges in the verses which follow:

He was oppressed; yet, in his affliction
He opened not his mouth.
Like a lamb led to the slaughter,
Like a sheep dumb before its shearers,
So he opened not his mouth. . . .
And his grave they made with the wicked,

With a rich man in his death.
Yet no violence had he done,
And there was no deceit in his mouth.
And yet it pleased Iahweh to bruise him.

Thus emerging from the Isaianic songs, two lines of Old Testament symbolism converge in Christ: the slaying of the paschal lamb and the ritual which commemorated this; and the symbolism of the obedient Servant of Iahweh whose death would be offered, like the ancient scapegoat, for the redemption of many. It is by a study of Isaias's doctrine against the background symbolism of the paschal lamb that we can see how the death of Jesus becomes a vicarious sacrifice in the Jewish sense. It is a sacrifice, therefore, whose essence is both immolation (as Lamb) and oblation (as Servant). It is unique in that a divinely appointed Man is the Victim; and its significance is such because that was what He intended it to be. Thus in the Cross, History and Symbol become one: Christ's historic gesture would not only symbolize redemption by sacrifice: it would achieve it. Now in the Last Supper Jesus replaced the paschal ritual by a new ceremony which was not only an eschatological banquet but would symbolize by word and gesture his historic act of Atonement. In the Bread and Wine there is present both Lamb and Victim-Servant; and by this presence the significance of the original sacrifice is renewed. The significance and the causality of the Cross are at once supernatural, corporate, and historico-symbolic.

But this messianic banquet—a ritual dimly echoed in the Dead Sea Scrolls—this celebration of the mysteries of the Lord until He come, is also the outward sign by which men could participate in the effects of the redemption; thus its causality as a liturgical ritual of commemoration must be analogous with the effectiveness of the Atonement itself. The Liturgy itself has its own peculiar Hebraic symbolism; for it does not merely incorporate the words of the Lord, but quotes them in a ritual narrative that enumerates the great acts of God towards men, culminating in the final Act, the Life, Passion and Death of the God-Man. As Jungmann and other modern liturgists have made clear, the kernel of the Liturgy is *narratio memorialis,* that is both eucharistic prayer and sacramental act. It is a distinctively Semitic kind of prayer to raise the heart of Iahweh by enumerating the past manifestations of His power; we see it very often in the Old Testament, and especially in the Book of Psalms; we see its origins in the victory songs of Miriam and Moses in Exodus 15:

> Iahweh is my strength and my song:
> Iahweh has become my salvation. . . .
> Pharaoh's chariots and his host
> Hath He cast into the sea.

Petition and thanksgiving by commemoration: this is Christianity's heritage from Moses. But the Mass as a memorial and commemoration of God's redeeming gesture not only symbolizes, it also achieves; and its causality is also historico-symbolic, though of a secondary order. The causality of the Church in the liturgy is corporate and mystical, though mediate, dependent and secondary.

So it is with all the other sacraments. They are all, in a sense, the mysteries of the Lord, commemorative of His life on earth. They are all in their special way symbols of participation in the graces of the Redemption; and, as such, their causality, though corporate and physical, is secondary and derivative. As symbolic gestures which dispense the graces of the Atonement they have a threefold reference: to Christ, to the Church, and to the individual participant. As rituals shared in by the faithful, they are tokens of decision, of assent and union; as sacred gestures of the Mystical Body the sacraments are signs of the Church's willingness to adopt and to incorporate, to seal and confirm, to reconcile the faithful soul in the specific way achieved by each sacrament. As ancient rites and formulae, they are cues to devotion and prayer as well as evidence of the Church's historic bond with the primitive catechesis and liturgy which came from her Lord.

We see, then, that symbolism is intimately connected with the central dogmas and the liturgy of Christianity. And it was this symbolism which became a fertile source of inspiration for the great poets and writers of the early Church. In the present study our aim will be to explore some of the more important areas of imagery and symbolism in which we can observe at close hand the subtle tension between theology and the Christian imagination. The subject is indeed a vast one, and we can only be selective. But by showing the growth of Christian poetic symbolism from the earliest days down to the Middle Ages it will be easier to undertake a provisory solution of the problem of the imagination and its place in the Christian kerygma. The answer, in a sense, is already implied from the beginning. But it cannot be a fully informed solution until we have seen the actual performance of the vast orchestra of imagery throughout the history of early Christian literature.

The Imagery of the New Testament

CHAPTER TWO

IF WE may distinguish between the "tenor" or doctrinal element of an image and the "vehicle" or more sensuous element, it becomes clear that many, indeed perhaps most, of the image-vehicles we find in the early Church in the presentation of the catechesis had already been suggested by the language of the Gospels and the Pauline epistles. The Godhead is compared with light and fire; grace is like fresh, spring water; the redemption is a ransoming by blood; the soul's struggle is a military warfare or an athletic contest with the Powers of Darkness; the apostolate is a fishing expedition on the sea; the growth of the Church is as a vine or a tree; the Lord is a bridegroom and the faithful are his bride.

Particularly striking are the images we find in the Gospel of St. John. The inaccessible light shines in the darkness but the darkness cannot comprehend it; yet the Powers of Darkness have their short reign, and we see the night enveloping the apostle Judas as he sets out on his traitorous mission. Connected with the light and darkness theme is the symbolism of vision-blindness, especially in the dramatic story of the man born blind. His final act of worship as his sight is restored has an obvious relevance for the new catechumens of the Johannine community: "Blessed are they who do not see and yet believe." There is the water-grace symbolism in the episode with the Samaritan woman at the well of her forefathers. And the symbol of water and blood gushing from the side of the Crucified is perhaps related to the imagery of the new dispensation as announced by Isaias, to the waters we are to draw with joy from the fountains of the Savior (*Is.* 12.3). Life, light, water, food—these are the basic symbols John uses to describe the redemptive work of Jesus.

Within these fertile images we see the seeds of later complex dogma; for, from the earliest times, the dramatic force of the Church's catechesis always operated strongly upon the imagination. In this, the apostolic Fathers and Christian writers only followed the example of Christ and His apostles. To observe this developing process more closely throughout the patristic period will be the burden of our subsequent chapters.

One of the most fruitful sources of kerygmatic imagery in the primitive Church was the corpus of epistles written by St. Paul. In a sense, it is easier to discuss Pauline imagery than to explain his doctrine. For even in the patristic period, though Paul's superb images of salvation always exercised a vigorous influence upon the Christian imagination, it cannot be said that his doctrines always enjoyed a unanimous interpretation. Even in the second epistle of Peter we read that in the letters of "our most dear brother Paul . . . there are certain things difficult to understand, which the unlearned and the unstable distort" (2 *Peter* 3.14). Many of the early Fathers, as for example Methodius, John Chrysostom, Augustine, wrestled with the subtleties of Paul's style and often admitted defeat. And surely it must be admitted that there is a certain violence and lack of logic in Paul's style, such that an analysis of the letters has troubled most if not all his commentators even from the second century of our era.

There is, indeed, more clarity in *Hebrews* and the three Pastoral letters, and this has been urged in support of the theory that they are not directly Pauline in authorship. As for the other letters, the difficulty in understanding Paul's apparent gaps in thought becomes less acute if we recognize the possibility of later editorial dislocation. This is in itself a not unlikely hypothesis in view of the nature of the epistles themselves and the haphazard publishing procedures of the early days of the Church. Thus it may be that *Romans* contains a fragmentary letter (from 16.1 on) of introduction on behalf of a Greek lady named Phoebe;

Philippians may comprise two letters, one (4.10–20) being a letter of thanks; and it has been suggested that the two epistles to Corinth are in reality fragments of four separate letters joined together for editorial convenience. But there still remain "certain things hard to be understood, which the unlearned and unstable wrest . . . to their own destruction" (2 *Peter* 3.16). But if St. Augustine in his *On Christian Doctrine* could apply the principles of Greco-Roman rhetoric in an effort to analyze Paul's style, an image-analysis might throw even more light on his vigorous, combative temperament and the unique focus of his Christian preaching.[8]

From the psychological point of view, the focal point of Paul's vivid imagery would seem to be the violent experience of his conversion. In one place (1 *Cor.* 15) he makes a parallel between the resurrection of the body—and, indeed, Christ's resurrection—and his own conversion. This is the ultimate grace that has made him what he is (1 *Cor.* 15.10). Just as the risen Christ was seen by Peter and the rest, so did he appear to Paul "as to a child untimely born." The word Paul uses here (*ektroma*) is a technical medical term for a child that is born dead because of a miscarriage or an abortion; the Latin word is *abortivus* or *abortus.* But the exact meaning that Paul attaches to the word is unclear. Some have interpreted it to mean that Paul was "untimely ripped from the bosom of the Synagogue." But the more usual meaning of the Greek word is "a child born dead," as some of the ancient lexica define it. In Latin, *abortivus* is used by Horace of a dwarf, or an abnormally small person. But the clue to the meaning of the image is that Paul is here contrasting himself with the other apostles and those who lived during Christ's lifetime. The primary meaning of the word here, therefore, is that Paul was not born (by faith) at the time of the other apostles; he was born in a different way. Not living as they did in the company of Christ, he did not have the time to mature, as an embryo should, but he was thrust out suddenly and violently into the new faith. The word is therefore accurately used: if birth refers to the faith,

[8] For a discussion of the imagination in St. Paul, see A. Brunot, *La génie littéraire de saint Paul* (Paris, 1955), esp. pp. 203 *ff.*, with my review in *Theological Studies* 17 (1956), 219–223.

then what Paul means is that he was deprived of the normal gestation period. This fits in perfectly with what he says later about spending only a few days with the apostles at Jerusalem. He is stressing the different way by which he came upon the truth. But the word may also be a term of opprobrium for one who is small or deformed. If Paul were, in addition, small of stature, the word would have taken on a special irony; but we cannot be sure. It does, in any case, stress the suddenness and violence of his conversion. It is thus at the root, in a sense, of all the symbolism that he used throughout his epistles.

Paul wrote as a great poet of early Christianity, and the violent imagery in which he clothes his revelation reflects the deep conflicts within his soul. Paul's change from persecutor to Christian was in itself a violent one: from Old Man to New, from Death to Life, was sudden. Truth came, in Paul's case, with a shock of recognition; and it is this violence that is, in part, at the root of much of his thought. Paul stresses the suddenness of his change in *Galatians* 1.15–16, and simply states that he spent three years in Arabia and in Damascus (*Gal.* 1.18) before he had any contact with the Apostles themselves in Jerusalem. From his own writings we are not sure what he did in Damascus; but King Aretas's soldiers pursued him, probably for an alleged breach of public order, and he himself testifies that he escaped from the city walls by being hidden somehow in a basket (2 *Cor.* 11.32). It was only afterwards that he spent a fortnight with the Apostles in Jerusalem (*Gal.* 1.18).

This simple, straightforward account, that we find mostly in *Galatians,* stands in sharp contrast to the dramatic portrait of the journey to Damascus which we find in the ninth chapter of *Acts.* There we are told the story of Paul's mission of persecution on behalf of the High Priest of Jerusalem. While riding on horseback (or, perhaps, in a chariot) in the direction of Damascus, Paul is thrown to the ground by a sudden light from heaven. And when, after hearing the voice of Jesus, he rises from the ground, he discovers that he is blind. It is, indeed, a psychic blindness, symbolic of the state of spiritual darkness in which Paul lived. We shall never be able to reconstruct the psychological shock which Paul suffered at this time, whether on the road to Damascus or elsewhere, but it is clear that the story of his conversion is told in *Acts* as a source of inspiration for the faithful: it is part of the primitive catechesis, even though Paul himself does not mention the incident on the road or the phenomenon of blindness.

But whether we study Paul's own version of his sudden change or follow the more picturesque account in *Acts,* it would seem that both reflect the violent and vigorous nature of the conversion: from blindness to vision, from persecutor to persecuted, from Damascus to Jerusalem. No other New Testament writer so clearly reveals his own personality in his writings and the ardent nature of his involvement in the Christian revelation. His epistles breathe an assurance, a boldness that carries all before it. And everywhere he puts forth the mark of authenticity: I have seen the Lord, I have been rapt to the third heaven, I have spoken with the Apostles, I preach Christ Crucified. There is no other wisdom than the folly of the Cross; no other message but Christ dying and risen again; and, if Christ be not risen, then is our faith in vain. Everywhere there is the fiery breath of inspiration—almost like the authentic tongues that descended upon those who waited in the upper room.

Leaving aside the *Epistle to the Hebrews,* as well as the other letters (*Ephesians* and the Pastorals) whose direct Pauline authorship is open to controversy, it is clear that the dominant symbol of Paul's writings is the dramatic clash or confrontation of opposites. Symbolically they express the violence he experienced in his conversion from Judaism, and the sharp, contrasting colors under which he saw the different periods of his own life and, by projection, the process of conversion for any Christian. On every page there is a personal statement, a sense of decision, a taking of a stand against the Old in favor of the New.

This basic antinomy in Paul is developed through a series of striking images. They are the pairs: Adam and Christ, the old man and the new, the spirit and the letter of the Law, Life and Death, walking in the day and the night in sobriety and drunkenness, acting like a child and like a man. For the faithful, the sacramental act which signifies this change is the dying to self in the waters of baptism and the emerging, the rising up with Christ. Once this great transition has been effected, there remains only to build up the Church, to struggle against the powers of darkness, and to wait for the Final Coming. The process of the building of the Church on earth is compared to the growth of a body —the body, indeed, of Christ—with members specialized for various functions. This image of the cosmic Christ, which is developed so magnificently in the epistle to the Ephesians, is one of the focal images of the Pauline writings. There is a mystic identification of Christ with His Church such that the faithful complete and complement His sufferings, and somehow fulfill the archetypal image of the Servant that was first truly verified in Jesus. The baptized are his members, the tools of justice, achieving the consummation that is to prepare for his Parousia.

Another favored image is the building or construction of a Temple, with Christ and the Apostles as the foundation stones. It is a Temple of the Spirit—and Paul himself is its architect (1 *Cor.* 3.10). Or again it is a planting (1 *Cor.* 3.7–9), as of the Lord's vineyard, and working as God's husbandmen until the time of vintage come. Again, the life of the Christian is a baking of bread, using fresh new leaven (1 *Cor.* 5.7), to prepare for a new Pasch, eating the unleavened bread of truth (1 *Cor.* 5.8). All of these activity-symbols—planting, growing, building, baking —suggest the excitement of working for the Kingdom, the glory of the goal, and the co-operation of willing workers. They are all images of social import, suggestive of the positive side of the new convert's life in Christ; they underline the more activist, voluntarist aspect of the Church.

There is also, in Paul, a small cluster of nuptial images which were to be more extensively developed later on by Origen and the Alexandrian school. In 1 *Corinthians* 7.34 he urges virgins to remain unmarried that they might give more attention to the Lord; from here the transition is easily made to Paul's espousal of the virgin Church in 2 *Corinthians* 11.2. Here Paul plays the role of the young bride's father or guardian in the Roman legal *sponsalia* or betrothal-ceremony. The prospective groom or his guardian would ask the girl's father: *Spondesne?* "Do you promise me your daughter?" And he would reply, *Spondeo,* "I do so promise." Sometimes gifts or pledges were then exchanged to seal the contract. So too Paul has promised to deliver his Church to Jesus, though the ultimate marriage has not been consummated. Again in *Ephesians* 5.25 husbands are commanded to love their wives as Christ loved the Church, and the very mystery of the marriage union (*Ephes.* 5.32) is taken as a symbol of the supernatural bond that exists between Jesus and those who have been sealed with his sacraments.

Jesus himself had suggested the comparison in his charming parable of the Wise and Foolish Virgins. There (*Mat.* 25.1–12) ten maidens are awaiting the marriage procession outside the bridegroom's house. When the groom would conduct his new bride from her father's house, he would be welcomed at the doors and then invite certain guests in to share in his wedding banquet. In the parable, the foolish maidens are not there when the wedding cortège arrives, and once the banquet has started the groom no longer wishes to be disturbed. The foolish or improvident virgins are shut out. In *Matthew* the marriage symbolism bears both a messianic and an eschatological connotation: the ready acceptance of Jesus' mission is also a foreshadowing of the marriage banquet of Heaven. Thus both in *Matthew* and in Paul we find the foundation for all the mystical nuptial imagery that will be developed in elaborate detail by the Alexandrian school against the background of an allegorical exegesis of the *Song of Songs* and the 44th (or epithalamian) Psalm.

Christ's comparison of his word to food and drink set in train a long tradition of very natural metaphors. Thus Paul in his first epistle to Corinth (3.2) says: I fed you not with meat but with milk, for you were not yet able to bear it. He regularly compares growth in Christ with physical maturity and the leaving of childish habits. The analogy is much clearer in *Hebrews* 5.12–14: they have need again, complains the inspired writer, of the milk of babes, and not the solid food of adults, because they have become "dull of hearing." Here the comparison is a pejorative one. But again in the first epistle of Peter (2.2), the Christians are babes newborn in innocence, craving the spiritual milk of the message of Jesus. From these passages there is a natural transition to the doctrine we find in Origen's *Homilies on Numbers* (hom. 27), where he distinguishes three types of diet corresponding to three levels of doctrine: (1) the milk diet of the infant; (2) the vegetarian diet for those of delicate health; and (3) the full-blooded diet of the healthy man and the athlete. It is only at the last level that we will find the subtle *gnosis,* or revelation of the secret mysteries of Christianity, normally hidden from those whose minds are too weak to penetrate the ultimate meaning of the Scriptures. After Origen the metaphor becomes more and more stereotyped in the patristic writers. In Methodius' *Banquet,* the actual dinner becomes a symbol of the Church's life on earth, foreshadowing the nuptial banquet of heaven. Even in Dante's *Convivio,* the "bread of angels" is served for all those who thirst after knowledge.[9]

But we have strayed somewhat from the simple metaphor of milk and solid food as we have found it in Paul. Another sequence of images concerns battle, athletic contests and the like. For Paul, however, the contest of Christianity is staged as a spectacle for all the world to behold (1 *Cor.* 49.9). But here he seems to have in mind in the word "spectacle" (*theatron*), the Roman amphitheatre, where the battles involved the real death of the gladiators themselves or of condemned criminals. The symbol of life as a kind of drama, inherited from Stoic-Cynic sources, is found in the later patristic writers, in Augustine, for example, Basil, Boethius, and others. For Paul, however, the important series of struggle-images embodies the profound need for self-conquest in the life of the Christian endowed with the grace of Jesus. One of the most striking of these image-clusters in Paul is that of the Christian's armor for the battle of the spirit. We find it first in 1 *Thess.* 5.8–9, a passage which may be modelled on *Isaias* 59.17. We must walk, says Paul, soberly by day, having the breastplate of faith and love and the helmet of hope. In the passage from Second Isaias it is Iahweh who puts on the clothes of vengeance, the cloak of zeal, with the breastplate of righteousness and the helmet of salvation. In the epistle to the Ephesians we find the imagery developed into a full-scale battle: against the principalities and powers, the spirits of wickedness. For this the Christian must don the armor of God (and again the Isaian

[9] See also E. R. Curtius, *European Literature and the Latin Middle Ages* (tr. by W. Trask, New York, 1953), pp. 134 *ff.*, with the literature there cited.

passage is implicit): there is the Isaian breastplate of righteousness and the helmet of salvation, the girdle of truth and the sandals of the gospel of peace, the shield of faith and the sword of the Spirit, in our fight against the darts of the Evil One. The battle is much more imaginatively conceived in *Ephesians* than in 1 *Thessalonians.* In the latter epistle we are armed with the theological virtues; and our struggle is not so much with the spirits of evil as with ourselves and with the implications of the Gospel message.

Closely linked with these are the athletic metaphors. The symbolism of crowns in Paul (1 *Cor.* 9.24 *ff.*; 1 *Tim.* 4.7–8; *cf. Phil.* 3.14) develops from the ancient practice of using crowns at feasts and banquets, as decorations for military prowess and as prizes in athletic contests. All three of these levels are present when Paul speaks of the crown as a reward. For the Christian the crown is the culmination of battle and contest, and it is the beginning of a heavenly banquet, the Messianic feast. Paul's most freqeunt metaphor, however, is the foot-race (1 *Cor.* 9.24–7; *Phil.* 3.13–14; 1 *Tim.* 4.7–8). It is for this strenuous race that we must restrain ourselves, so as to keep in training (1 *Cor.* 9.25). Here too there is the symbol of the constant stretching forward, the straining for victory and the ultimate prize (*Phil.* 3.13–14). Then there is the striking boxing metaphor (1 *Cor.* 9.27): Paul's boxing is not mere shadow-boxing, but (by a curious use of words) he says he bruises himself, in order to bring his body into subjection. The Greek words used here are very strong: I bruise (*hupopiazo*) my body, and treat it as a slave (*doulagogo*); and, though we cannot be entirely sure, some form of physical self-chastisement or even (as we find in the lives of the later hermits) the wearing of bonds and shackles may be implied. The violence of Paul's conversion may ultimately have issued in some form of self-inflicted pain.

There is a reference to wrestling with evil spirits in *Ephesians* (though the battle and athletic metaphors elsewhere refer to *internal* struggles), and oddly enough, there is a reference to the uselessness of physical exercise in 1 *Tim.* 4.8, which is quite unlike St. Paul. But there are implicit images of battle and struggle in 1 *Tim.* 6.12 and 2 *Tim.* 4.7–8.

These three groups of images are the most important for Pauline thought: images of dynamic contrast as the flesh and the spirit, life and death; images of progress and growth, of planting and building; and images of warfare, training and struggle. All deal with the Christian life under different aspects: as conversion, as confident growth, and, finally, under its more difficult aspect of the curbing of lower tendencies.

Another important image, which deals rather with man's relationship to God, is that of the potter and the vessel. In *Romans* 9, Paul speaks of the mystery of the divine predestination, and how it happened that only a few Israelites actually received the message of Jesus. Thus he adapts a passage from Isaias (45.9) in which Iahweh is made to proclaim His supremacy over creation and the wisdom of His designs. In Isaias the clay asks the Potter: What makest Thou? In Paul (*Rom.* 9.20–21), the Potter makes two sorts of vessels, vessels of wrath and vessels of mercy—those who were called to the Gospel and those who were not—and they may not ask the divine Artisan, Why hast Thou made me thus? Paul has changed the image from one of divine omnipotence to one of election and predestination, with enormous consequences for the future history of theology. For the problem of predestination arises rather from our human conception of the divine dominion than from the dominion itself. But, in any case, the image of the potter and the vessel should not deceive us into denying the role of human freedom in the determination of man's ultimate beatitude.

In the last place we may group together all of Paul's eschatological images: the final coming, the resurrection and the happiness of heaven. The symbol of the potter is, for Paul, merely an analogy, although a useful one. Later, in the hands of Fathers like Methodius of Olympus it will serve to explain the mysteries of the Incarnation, Redemption, and the creation of the human soul. Methodius, of course, as a Platonist adapts the potter-image by blendng it with the Platonic Craftsman or Demiurge, the demi-god who fashioned the world. In Paul, however, it is still a haunting symbol of resignation to the inscrutable world-plan of the Godhead. In this sense, it is perhaps his most profound metaphor: for in it are embodied all the other mysteries which so affected him, the wisdom of God's plan of Redemption and the struggle with the daemonic powers within man's soul. Even though not so explicit as we find it in the later Fathers, the image already enshrouds the secret of God's way with men, and the need of humility before the divine omnipotence.

The classic picture of the Final Coming is given in the first epistle to the Thessalonians. The Lord Himself will come down from heaven with a cry (1 *Thess.* 4.16), with a trumpet sound and the voice of the archangel. The just will be caught up into the heavens with Christ, to live forever with Him in heaven. Once again, in 1 *Corinthians* 15.51 *ff.*, Paul speaks of this scene, stressing the appearance of the new, risen bodies with which the dead shall be clothed. At the sound of a trumpet—the usual signal in ancient times for assemblies either of soldiers or citizens—the dead will be raised incorruptible, and we shall be changed. Again, the longing, the groaning, for this final day, for the building of the eternal tabernacle, is developed in 2 *Corinthians* 5.1–4. Indeed, all of creation awaits that day (*Rom.* 8.21–3). The picture is completed in the second epistle of Peter (3.10–12), where we are told that earth and heaven will dissolve in fire and a new habitation will be prepared for the just. Here again it is Paul who attempts to give a more Platonic dimension to the life of the blessed in heaven: for there we shall see the Lord in person, face to face; there will be no place for faith or hope, but only love (1*Cor.* 13.12–13).

Indeed, his vision of the future Coming would seem to be in part a projection of his own mystical experience around the time of his conversion. It was, he says a vision, a revelation of the Lord (2 *Cor.* 12.1 and 7), in which he was caught up into paradise, into the "third heaven." The ancients believed in three levels above the earth: the air (or *aër*), or atmosphere around the earth; the *aether*, or the realm beyond that, in which the stars and planets were; and, finally, the last part of the heavens, where they placed the abodes of the gods and blessed. It was here that Paul, in a kind of transport, heard the words "that no man may utter." Here, indeed, in a vision that seems very much like the recorded experiences of the mediaeval mystics, we have the foundation for Paul's doctrine. On this historic phenomenon—

and, of course, on his own peculiar temperament—was grounded the ecstatic and sometimes violent imagery we find throughout his works. In particular, it may be that his vision of the Final Coming and the rising of the blessed was a projection of his experience. As he was swept up to the third heaven, so will the just on the last day; as he received vision and revelation, so will they be with Christ, seeing the Lord face to face in perfect charity, with hope and faith now dissolved in blessed union. This was the ultimate dissolution that he longed for: to be dissolved and to be with Christ. Indeed, all the symbols Paul uses for the Christian experience may well be projections of his own struggle and ecstasy, of the violent ups and down, of his own Christian experience: he is nailed to the Cross with Christ, and at once struggling with the goad of the flesh, the messenger from Satan (2 *Cor.* 12.7). Paul is the first true ecstatic of the primitive Church. And his beautiful, violent imagery suggests that his was a deeply poetic, even ecstatic temperament.

The Pauline portrait of the Final Coming was developed in many ways by the ecclesiastical writers, especially by the so-called Millenarists, who believed that Christ would reign on earth in glory over His Church for a thousand years. Among these were Commodian the poet, Lactantius, Justin Martyr, Victorinus, Irenaeus, and Methodius of Olympus. There is an especially striking picture of the Millenium in Lactantius' *Epitome of the Divine Institutes* (§ 72). "The heavens will be opened in the dead of night," he tells us, "and then Christ will come down to earth in great majesty, preceded by a cloud of fire and a legion of angels." Then will the Prince of Darkness be bound and cast into a dungeon, and Christ will deliver all the blessed to a Holy City. Then, according to the tradition, Saturn's golden age will be restored:

> Honey will drip from stones, springs of milk and wine will flow, and all wild beasts will be tamed; the wolf will wander innocently among the sheep, the calf will feed with the lion, the dove will share with the hawk, and the snake will lose its venom.

But at the end of the Millenium, according to Lactantius, there will be a new cataclysm as the Beast is once more unchained;

the just will lie hidden underground while God rains brimstone on the sinners and while they fight and murder among themselves. After this,

> There will be an earthquake. The mountains will be cloven, and the valleys drawn down into the abyss, and the bodies of all the dead will be collected in a place called Polyandrion, "the place of many men."

Then only will God clothe the just with angelic shapes, and deliver the wicked to the fire of perpetual torment. It is a moving portrayal, but an incredibly confused one: the double resurrection of the just is even more difficult to follow in the full-length version of the story in the *Institutes,* of which the *Epitome* is an abridgement. The two traditions, pagan and Christian, have in Lactantius come together in violent confusion.

In contrast with the body of Paul's writings, *Hebrews* and the Pastorals reflect a markedly different sequence of images.[10] The Pastorals have very little vigorous imagery. In 1 *Timothy* there is a brief mention of battle (6.12), and the symbol of Light as the abode of the Godhead (6.16); in 2 *Timothy* the author speaks of the spreading canker-sore of heresy (2.17); and the Pauline athletic and race-course imagery recurs (2.5, 4.7–8), with the Lord as the referee to award the crown of champions. In *Hebrews,* on the other hand, the symbolism is quite unique and all pervasive: the Kingdom is compared to a Mosaic Temple, in which Christ is the High Priest performing the ritual sacrifice. The development is initiated from chapter three (1–4), and culminates in the fine Mosaic image of Sinai and the Heavenly Jerusalem in chapter twelve (18–19, 22). The *Epistle to the Hebrews* is, in truth, a carefully developed treatise on the sacrificial aspects of Christ's Life and Death; and the entire tone of the work is rabbinical, Mosaic, and ritualistic. There is a fine image of the earth, blessed and fruitful, nourishing mankind in 6.7–8, and a very Pauline comparison of doctrine to the milk of

[10] For some of the problems connected with the New Testament epistles, see A. Robert and A. Feuillet, *Introduction à la Bible* (2 vols., Tournai, 1957), II.515 *ff.* (L. Cerfaux, J. Cambier, J. Cantinat), with the relevant bibliography.

bases and the solid food of men (5.11–14). The ritual imagery of the Temple and the Holy of Holies was especially favored by the Greek Fathers, like Methodius and Gregory of Nyssa. But it is quite unlike what we expect from Paul, and was obviously intended for an audience more deeply imbued with Judaic ways of thinking and praying.

The three epistles of John are not noted for their imagery. 1 *John,* however, reiterates some of the symbols of the Fourth Gospel, as the walking in Light and in Darkness (1 *John* 1.6–7); and the water and blood (5.6), referring perhaps to Christ's Baptism and Death, as well as to the water and blood that came from his side on the Cross, as a witness of his messianic mission. The two Petrine letters are quite alive with vigorous imagery, although each is markedly different. In 1 *Peter* we have the lovely picture of newborn babes thirsting for their mother's milk (2.2); then there is the building and temple imagery (2.5), with living stones, and Christ the keystone as well as the stone of stumbling for the wicked (2.6–8). Others are the dressing images implied in girdling the loins (1.13), and the contrast between inner and outer adornment (3.3–4). On the other hand, 2 *Peter* has very meagre imagery, except that used in the diatribe (or series of woes or curses) against heretics and false prophets in 2.12–22. It is a violent and picturesque sequence that would have done justice to an Archilochus. This sort of diatribe, clothed in sharply focused metaphors, we shall also see in James and Jude. In 2 *Peter,* 2.12–22, no qualifier is too gross to describe these doctors of iniquity: they are mere animals fit for destruction, adulterous and covetous; they are springs without water, mists driven before a storm; they are like dogs returning to their vomit, and sows that wallow in the mire.

There is a similar diatribe in Jude 10–16: the ungodly men that are trying their best to pervert the just are creatures without reason, they are the hidden rocks among the love-feasts, shepherds that only feed themselves, clouds without water carried by the winds, fruitless trees of autumn, wild sea waves, wandering stars. The language is very much like that of 2 *Peter.* The epistle of James has a brief diatribe against the rich (5.1–6): their garments are moth-eaten, and their gold and silver are rusted—a splendid example of visual execration. Again, the wealthy man is like the flower of the grass that withers with the rising sun and the wind (1.11); the doubter, like the surge of the sea driven by the wind (1.6). The man who receives the good news of the Gospel but does not act upon it is like a man who looks at himself in a mirror (1.23–4). The meaning of the simile is manifold: on the first level it suggests that the man without good works has an impermanent, vague, and temporary contact with Christianity; his status is unreal, like the temporary image in the mirror, which, as the author asserts, can be so easily forgotten. On the second level, however, the simile suggests the selfish narcissism of the man who gazes at himself, and his forgetting what he looks like implies that he does not see how truly ugly he is. The image is quite unique in Scripture, and may perhaps have overtones of the Narcissus story: Narcissus died of love of his own image reflected in the water of a fountain; hence the story often implies the pathos of frustrated love and death. There is a very interesting bit of imagery in *James* 3.2–7 dealing with the avoidance of faults and with self-control. Men control horses by small bits, tame the animals of the field, and guide ships through the sea by a steering-oar. They should therefore be able to control the tongue. But the examples might well be taken from Sophocles' play, *Antigone;* for there the Chorus speaks of man's power over the seas and animals (332 *ff.*), and the curbing of horses with the bit (477). The comparisons could, of course, be entirely traditional, but they are indications of the remarkable vitality and imagination that we find in the epistle of James.

Here is not the place to deal with the problems of the *Apocalypse* of John, which obviously go far beyond the realm of symbolism and imagery.[11] But the mystery is that anyone—even the audience for whom it was first intended—could ever have understood it. The Fathers in general are quite at variance in their

[11] See the discussion by M. E. Boismard, *Introduction à la Bible,* II.709–42; and for the connection between the Woman and the Virgin Mary, see pp. 737 *f. Cf.* also my commentary, *St. Methodius: The Symposium: A Treatise on Chastity* (Ancient Christian Writers 27, London and Westminster, Md., 1958), pp. 109–116, 223. On the Apocalypse see further, S. Giet, *L'Apocalypse et l'histoire* (Paris, 1957), whose approach differs sharply from mine.

interpretations; and even Methodius, who spends so much of his *Symposium* on the Woman of *Apocalypse* 12, clearly reflects the confusions and contradictions which prevailed during the early patristic period. The truth would seem to be that the *Apocalypse,* as the result of a prolonged transport or series of ecstasies, has no unique interpretation. It is a symbolic message that has become disordered by the overpowering onslaught of religious enthusiasm; hence, though its total meaning is clear, it is impossible to give a satisfactory account of many details.

Its mode of communication is almost pre-logical, as though it were a vast mosaic or a musical cult hymn of enthronement. Indeed, it is perhaps the musical imagery we find throughout that is the real clue to the meaning of the book: it is a New Song to the Lamb (*Apoc.* 5.9; *cf.* 15.3–4). Everywhere there are short hymns and acclamations, accompanied by the sounds of harps and angelic trumpets and flutes (5.8, 8.2, 18.2, and elsewhere). Ostensibly it is a vision of what is "shortly to come to pass" (1.1), a prophetic vision of the Last Things to restore the Seven Churches to their pristine fervor. Yet once the basic symbolic scene is set in the great throne-room of the Lamb, the apocalypse of the world to come is insensibly fused with a vision of the Church's struggle against the powers of iniquity, the Dragon and the Whore of Babylon, while the Word of God strides victorious on his steed as the King of Kings and Lord of Lords. It is only in the final chapters that the towers of the heavenly Jerusalem emerge, and the rivers of paradise flow once more from the throne. But apart from the vivid and terrifying visual imagery, the most pervasive symbol would seem to be that of horses, dragons, and other animals, and this offers a clue to the unique imaginative genius of the inspired writer. The dragons and other horrible beasts are, of course, embodiments of evil, terror, the forces of the unconscious and the malign that threatens the just from within and without. They represent all that is irrational and revolting in the world, corruptive and destructive of the good. The white steeds, however, are symbols of masculine majesty, vitality, strength, and purity (6.2, 19.11, 19.14); on them ride the Word and his numberless armies, to do battle with the Beast.

Two important complementary images are the Woman clothed

with the sun (12.1), who would seem to represent the Church as a Mother, and the Harlot (17.1) with whom the kings of the world have committed fornication. They represent the two opposing principles of life, Good and Evil, as two sources of attraction and centers of activity. In the one we see embodied all the wholesomeness of motherhood, in the other all the wiles and seductions of the Evil One. The type of the wicked woman is common in Hebrew literature from the days of Hosee (2.5), for whom fornication and lewdness is an image of the people's unfaithfulness to Iahweh (6.10). In the book of Proverbs is the classic denunciation of the woman whose lips drop honey (*Prov.* 5.3 *ff.*),

> And her mouth is smoother than oil,
> But in the end she is bitter as wormwood,
> Sharp as a two-edged sword.
> Her feet go down to death,
> Her steps take hold on Sheol.

The good Woman of the *Apocalypse,* on the other hand, probably derives from the female figure of Wisdom, *Hokmah,* in *Proverbs* (9.1 *ff.*) and in the other Wisdom-books. In the *Apocalypse,* however, both female figures have been transformed: and if the Woman crowned with the stars suggests the Virgin Mary, at least by indirection, the Harlot certainly refers to Rome, mistress of the world, seated among the seven hills.

The *Apocalypse* is indeed the Christian counterpart of the document found among the Dead Sea Scrolls entitled *The War of the Sons of Light and the Sons of Darkness.*[12] But even apart from its Christian theological dimension, the *Apocalypse* is a far more beautiful, more stirring piece of work. As a mystical vision the *Apocalypse* oscillates between symbols of confidence and sheer terror, love and violent disgust, attraction and sickening revulsion. On another level it can be taken as a long doxological hymn, a song of awe and terror at the dominion of Christ and the world, and the violent struggle his Church must endure as it awaits his Final Coming in a hostile world.

[12] See, for example, the version given by Theodor H. Gaster, *The Dead Sea Scriptures in English* (Garden City, N. Y., 1956). pp. 281 *ff.*, with the notes.

The actual text of the inspired author, John, exiled for his love of Jesus to the island of Patmos, is full of insoluble difficulties. Some sections, in the view of scholars, appear to have been completed during the reign of Nero (A.D. 54–68); others, and perhaps the final edition itself, under the reign of Domitian (81–96). Both these emperors persecuted the Christians and both evoked the minatory and prophetic message of the series of visions. In some verses the author seems dependent on Ezechiel; in others on Joel and Daniel. Some scholars would attempt to divide the text into various strata, attributed to various hands. But perhaps the best view is to take the book as a series of ecstatically induced visions or hallucinations, without special order or chronology; much of the material is derivative, much of it is used within the book more than once. It is a prophecy of the sort that Paul mentions in his first epistle to the Corinthians (14.1–5).

We are grateful that this unique record was preserved: it was a charism that was not long to endure in the primitive Church. But despite the disorders of the visions, the ultimate message of the *Apocalypse* stands clear. God, true to His promise in the Old Law, will first try the enemies of His Church and then finally destroy them. The Woman will escape unharmed with her Child, and the Beast will finally be crushed. Rome will be destroyed by conquerors from the East and a long new era of triumph will be established. In the end, after a final assault by the Evil One, the walls of the Heavenly Jerusalem will rise, and God "will wipe all tears from their eyes." Fittingly does this celestial vision close the inspired pages of the New Testament: it was a symbolic glimpse of heaven which was to draw innumerable saints, poets, and ecstatics to heights of supreme creativity and personal achievement.

Hermas and the Apostolic Fathers

CHAPTER THREE

THE EPISTLE of Pope Clement was written to settle a dispute which arose in the Christian community of Corinth some time during the persecution of Domitian (A.D. 95–6). The liturgical prayer at its close, and certain later references, suggest that it was intended to be read during the sacred liturgy; and its fame was such that it continued to be read in other churches even after the cessation of the Corinthian trouble which was its occasion. What the original sedition was, we know not; but Clement's letter breathes such a majesty of tone, a sense of peace and obedience, that it must surely have achieved its purpose.

The three most important symbols that occur in the letter strongly reinforce the general theme. The first is the harmony and order of the entire universe, a topic derived from the Stoics' discussion of the Natural Law. Clement sees nature as a series of harmonious movements: the seasons, the seas, the land and its vegetation, the planets. Even the animals share in this organic unity, meeting as they do in concord and peace (1 *Clem.* 20). Man alone, he seems to suggest, is able to withdraw from the harmony by sin and disorder, as have the seditious Christians of Corinth. Another symbol of order, now on the human level, is his comparison of the Church to an army (37.1–3). In an efficient army, not all can be commanders or centurions or corporals; but the ordinary soldier in the ranks must carry out their orders if the army is to be victorious. It is an image that recalls the violent battle metaphors of the *Apocalypse* and Paul; but as a symbol of order it occurs here for the first time. In the same passage (37.5) Clement also refers to the Pauline comparison of the Church to a body (1 *Cor.* 12.20–21), emphasizing once again the importance of what may seem to be unimportant members, and the necessity of co-operation. Clement's final image is one of hope and confidence: it is the mythical phoenix rising immortally out of its own ashes (25), much as we find it referred to by Herodotus and Pliny the Elder. It is Clement's attempt to soothe the discouragement of the disheartened Corinthians, and it reveals his deep understanding of their emotional needs in the problem at hand. The hope of immortality is ultimately the foundation for the Christian's belief in the harmony of the world and the moral order which man should bring into his own existence. Thus the first epistle of Clement, apart from its immediate purpose, is in its way a profound expression of the meaning of the Atonement: it is the bringing of order and harmony to a universe in which man is the noblest creation.

In our entire discussion of the imagery of the writers of the early Church, it must be borne in mind that their metaphors are not, for the most part, literary embellishment, but chosen purely for the sake of doctrinal illustration. The vast bulk of the literature of this period is primarily didactic or, rather, catechetical. Whether the medium was the treatise for private reading or the homily delivered during the sacred liturgy, the aim would be always the same: *kerygma* and *didache,* dogmatic and moral instruction. What images were chosen, however, is all the more interesting to us in as much as they were not consciously developed; rather they emerged from the Church's primitive consciousness as the most apt vehicle of dogma in the concrete circumstances. We must not then be surprised if the images in a particular work seem to lack coherence or reflect hasty thinking or random choice. At the same time it will be instructive for us to notice the growth and dominance of special symbols at different times in the Church's history. Indeed, one of the most striking symbolic works of this period, after the *Apocalypse,* is the curious book known as the *Shepherd.*

The *Shepherd* of Hermas was one of the most widely read books of early Christianity. One of the Greek manuscripts has come down to us in the great Codex Sinaiticus of the Bible, tacked on after the canonical books with the so-called *Epistle of Barnabas.* The distribution of the manuscripts of the Latin versions, and of the Coptic, Ethiopic, and Middle Persian versions, reveals how far the text of Hermas had spread throughout Egypt, Europe, and Asia. Tertullian, Origen, and Irenaeus were among those who considered the book to be inspired. At any rate, the *Shepherd,* as we have it, would appear to be a mosaic work, the result of a number of grafts on an original parent stem. And, as it spread, it became a kind of Christian *Volksbuch,* or chapbook, that was almost felt to be communal property as it circulated, acquiring variants and modifications.

It is no longer clear whether the very name Hermas is authentic or was simply adopted, as in the case of pseudo-Dionysius the Areopagite, to make the work seem to come from the entourage of St. Paul. My own guess is that the final redactor, who flourished perhaps under Trajan, was an Italo-Greek lay preacher from the region about Naples. Indeed, the suggestion of the Muratorian Canon, that the author was a kinsman of Pius I, Bishop of Rome about the middle of the second century, may not be far from the truth. But the attempt to pass off the apocalypse as a work of the apostolic period, the odd assortment of strange and sometimes erotic visions, the rigorist doctrine of guilt and repentance, all this would suggest that in Hermas we have a somewhat unbalanced, perhaps frustrated Christian teached with mediumistic tendencies. Most of the imagery seems to have been drawn from Hermas' waking or sleeping dreams; and the literary framework of many of the visions introduces the author reclining or sleeping (*Vision* 2.4, 3.1, etc.). The various levels in Hermas' work are: (1) apparently authentic ecstatic experience; (2) the sleeping dream, endowed by the writer with dogmatic importance; (3) the waking dream; and finally, (4) the purely literary vision or dream. On the fourth level, the vision or hallucination would merely be a literary framework created by the writer in order to invest his personal ideas with the atmosphere of authenticity. It is impossible for us now to recover the exact method or combination of methods used by Hermas in writing his work or by those, perhaps, who recorded it for him.

There is no organic unity discernible in the *Shepherd.* Even its main theme is partially obscured by the innumerable minor threads which the author was moved to develop. Indeed, the cause of this very obscurity may be the compilatory nature of the work. The primary theme is a call to penitence for all those who have committed serious sin after baptism; they must hasten to repent if they would not be shut out of the Tower of salvation (Similitudes 10.4.4). But there are a number of secondary themes, as for example, a more rigorous view of sin: every act that a man does out of pleasure is harmful (Similitudes 6.5.5); other themes are the virtues to be practiced by the just, and the manner by which the Church grows in the word, expressed by Hermas in a number of picturesque parables. On the other hand, the psychological stimulus for the work—at least for the first part—would seem to be Hermas' own guilt-feelings, whether because of a love of his owner, the lady Rhoda, who purchased him as a slave at Rome, or for some other reason. Though he protests his innocence in his work, it may be that in truth Hermas had reason for anxiety. As the work develops, however, this general atmosphere of guilt and the need of penance is extended to Hermas' own wife and children, his household, and finally the entire Church. Clement (presumably the first Pontiff of this name) is requested to publish Hermas' work throughout the churches of the Mediterannean area. Some scholars have felt that this part of the work is due to an earlier stratum which actually goes back to the days of Clement, that is, about the year A.D. 95. But it may very well be that the author Hermas, however much he may have adapted earlier sources, actually produced his work under Trajan but preferred to pass it off as an apocalypse of the Apostolic period. His purpose would therefore be much the same as the later Dionysius the Areopagite. Indeed, this hypothesis fits in with the general bizarre quality of the entire work.

The Shepherd could just as well have been called *The Ancient Lady,* for the feminine symbolism is much more important for the meaning of the whole. This symbolism radiates from the initial stimulus, from the lady Rhoda of Rome, and finally culminates in the Twelve Maidens who are to dwell as sisters in the house of Hermas. The fundamental imagery is largely erotic, and the entire work can perhaps be analyzed as a series of anxiety dreams.

Hermas' anxiety about impure thoughts—which is the psychological core of the work—is gradually extended to other areas, the attitude towards his own wife, to second marriages, overeating and fasting, doubts on faith, and apostasy.

Hermas' Ancient Lady, the *presbytera,* appears at first in a dream-sequence holding a codex containing the mandate she is to give him, arousing expectations that are not fulfilled. In subsequent apparitions she is seen in three forms, becoming by degrees more youthful and beautiful. The exact significance of this transformation is unclear. As an aged woman, she represents the wisdom of the Church, being derived either from the Woman of the Apocalypse or, if some modern commentators are right, the Cumaean Sibyl. In any case, her gradual change suggests the eternal youth of the Christian Church—and, in the specific context, symbolizes the renovation of the faithful which Hermas is preaching by means of second repentance. The aged Sibyl of *The Shepherd* foreshadows the dignified matron who appears to Boethius under the form of Philosophia. In the *Consolation* she is described as "full of years, but of inexhaustible vitality," sometimes appearing as of human size, at other times with her head touching the heavens. A similar archetypal Woman is found in the *Banquet* of Methodius: there she is the virgin Arete, a woman of great beauty, who welcomes the other virgins to her table under the chaste tree, and is obviously the symbol of Mother Church, the Spouse of Christ. The type becomes somewhat frequent in the Middle Ages, and its most successful evolution is seen in Dante's Beatrice.

Hermas' work would have enjoyed a denser unity if he had retained the mysterious virgin-figure throughout. From the Fifth Vision on, the scene is dominated by the mysterious Shepherd, after whom the book is named: it is the Angel of Repentance (Mandates 12.4.7), suggesting in his demeanor the Good Shepherd of the Fourth Gospel. But apart from those personifications, the most stirring images in Hermas are the sterile and fruitful trees, the symbol of the great Willow, the Tower of the Church, the Beast of iniquity, the twelve mountains of Arcadia, and the knots of good and evil ladies who reappear throughout the work.

The tree-symbolism suggests the life and growth of the

Church and its members: there is the heavy vine, the sterile elm, the Willow Tree; and these seem to be derived from the parables of the Gospel, the vine and its branches, the sterile fig tree, and the growing mustard-seed. There are overtones of the Old Testament shrubs and the trees of good and evil in the garden of Paradise. Hermas thus anticipates the complex botanical exegesis of the Alexandrian school, which developed out of Philo. But Hermas' contribution is unremarkable; for even the symbol of the Willow, which is original with the *Shepherd*, fails to be illuminating, succeeding only in being trite and dull.

More interesting is the figure of the Beast, an obvious imitation of the terrifying symbols of John's Apocalypse. The scene occurs in Vision Four, while Hermas is travelling along the Via Campagna which went from Capua to Cumae. In a thick dust storm, suggestive of the blinding powers of Darkness, Hermas suddenly sees a horrible Beast. It is a monster one hundred feet long, built like a whale, with a head like a huge vase; fiery locusts stream disgustingly from its maw. The great beast is perhaps a reminiscence of the Leviathan of the book of Job or the great fish of Jonas, and the fiery locusts suggest the Egyptian plagues of the Mosaic Exodus. The colors, black, fiery and bloody, gold and white, intensify the tone of phantasmagoria, and perhaps recall the coloring of the four horses of the *Apocalypse*. Hermas confronts the beast and it is destroyed after doing no more than stick out its tongue. The climax, unconsciously humorous, is trivial. It is a childish nightmare vision of Evil, and ends without point or significance.

The longest allegory of the book is the building of the great Tower, or Fortress, of the Church. It is erected by six young men (who are the angels first created by God to guard his handiwork) directly over the sea with stones taken from land and sea. Four types of stones are set: those symbolizing (1) the Apostles and the hierarchy, (2) those who have suffered martyrdom, (3) those who have kept the commandments, (4) those still young in the faith and not yet perfect. Eight types of stones are rejected, though they may still be used in the Tower: they are Christians who have seriously sinned, or else men who have refused to belong to the Church. Supporting this Fortress built over the waters—reminding us perhaps of the walking of Peter and Christ on the sea of Galilee—are seven women, but these shall be discussed farther on. The tower image is, again, dull and stereotyped, and derives most of its vitality from the building metaphors of Paul and 1 *Peter*. The "stone that the builders rejected," however, is now transformed to suit the needs of Hermas' doctrine on second repentance.

We have a hint of pastoral imagery in Hermas' picture of Arcadia. In the Ninth Similitude, Hermas is transported to Arcadia, to what he calls "a breast-shaped mountain" surrounded by a plain and twelve other mountains. The twelve mountains represent the nations of the world, like the twelve tribes of the Apocalypse. On the plain is a great white rock about which are gathered twelve maidens. On this another Tower is to be built; and the vision would seem to be largely a repetition of the picture of the Tower on the Via Campagna in Vision Three. Again the six young men appear, apparently the same angels who were mentioned in the earlier vision. The explanation of the meaning of the twelve mountains in Similitude 9.19 *ff*. is new but uninteresting. The exegesis of the different types of stones can only suggest the view that Hermas was keenly interested in stones and building—though he explicitly says he was not a stone-cutter. In any case, what for him was a dramatic vision seems to us now altogether trite if not positively confusing.

When all is said, it would appear that Hermas' most striking imagery is drawn from the women who inhabit his home and his dreams. Rhoda is transformed into the Ancient Lady; and the Lady, in turn, becomes a bride ready for marriage. In the second part, where the male figure of the Shepherd dominates the scene, we see different groups of allegorical females. Seven women support the first Tower of Vision Three: Faith, Temperance, Simplicity, Innocence, Sobriety, Knowledge, and Love. The sources for Hermas' good women are, in general, the theological virtues, the seven gifts of the Spirit (or the messianic virtues) mentioned in Isaias, and the Pauline fruits of the Holy Spirit (*Galatians* 5.22). The evil women are perhaps modelled on the Harlot of Babylon of the *Apocalypse*, and their vices are the opposite of the virtues or else are derived from Paul's list of the fifteen works of the flesh in *Galatians* 5.20–21. To portray them all as women in various functions is original with Hermas, and this is perhaps the most striking aspect of his work; it is here that he foreshadows Prudentius, mediaeval allegory, and the conceptions of Dante and Boccaccio. Jung, in his *Psychological Types,* has an entire section dealing with the "transition from the service of Woman to the service of the Soul";[13] and if in Jungian psychology the female dream-figure is a presentation of the Anima, in Freudian terminology it can, apart from erotic connotations, be a symbol of the superego. In any case, with Hermas' allegorical women we are at the heart of the most significant part of his work.

Of the evil women we are soon to hear. In Mandates 9–10 we learn that the Devil has three daughters, Double-Mindedness or Hypocrisy, Depression, and Irascibility. Double-Mindedness is, of course, the general fault which embodies the primitive concept of bad will, unwillingness to co-operate with the graces of the Atonement; it is the root of all wickedness among those Christians who have fallen after baptism. The other vices will be numbered among the Twelve Evil Women whom Hermas meets again during his mystical sojourn in Arcadia.

In Arcadia, around the door of the white rock over which the Tower of the Church is to rise, stand Twelve Good Maidens; five of these seem to be derived from Paul's list of the fruits of the Spirit in *Galatians;* others derive from the Isaian list of the seven messianic gifts. The Maidens assist the six angelic youths in the construction of the Tower; later they clean out the dirt and refuse from the Tower with brooms (Similitude 9.9.3). Soon after, Hermas is left alone with them, but is warned that he is to sleep with them as with sisters. After kissing him chastely, they begin a choral dance; then he sleeps upon their chitons as they are laid out as coverlets about the Tower. The next morning, the Shepherd explains that the maidens are the various Powers of the Son

[13] *Psychologische Typen* (Zurich, 1937), pp. 315 *ff. Cf.* also Maud Bodkin, *Archetypal Patterns in Poetry* (Oxford, 1934), pp. 174 *ff.* For a discussion of Hermas and the literature of this early period, one must consult J. Quasten, *Patrology,* vol. I (Westminster, 1950), and especially in the latest French edition, *Initiation aux Pères de l'Eglise* (Paris, 1955), I.49 *ff.,* with the bibliography.

of God; and that all the just must be clothed with their raiment. As Hermas frolics and plays with them, he seems to grow young again (Similitude 9.11.5); it is a pagan revel, an all-night festival vigil; but now Hermas has transformed it into an allegory of Christian living. He also receives a vision of the Twelve Evil Women who are connected with the rejected stones: they are Apostasy, Incontinence, Calumny, Hatred, Deceit, Licence, and the rest. They are clothed in black, with their shoulders bare and their hair down; for all their beauty, Hermas sees that they are cruel, overpowering all those that fall in love with them. Finally, in the Tenth Similitude, Hermas is bidden to live with the Twelve Good Maidens. In an enigmatic ending an Angel comes to take the Maidens and the Shepherd away, but promises that they will all return to Hermas' house later on.

Some minor imagery reinforces the general trend of the work: various beds, litters, and thrones, with attendant young men, the white wool of the Lady's chair, her tapping of Hermas on the chest in a gesture of lower-class familiarity (*Vis.* 2.4.2), the image of the book, various types of fruit- and tree-imagery. A curious passage occurs in Mandates 11.19: the Shepherd asks Hermas to try to squirt water through a siphon as high as the sky, "to see if you can make a hole in the heavens." It is a parable of the futility of earthly or daemonic power; but, as much else in the *Shepherd,* the image is drawn from the daily life of Hermas and the classes for whom the work is intended. The siphon or syringe was used for piping water by suction for irrigating plants and vines in the Mediterranean area.

Despite the general incoherence of the work, its general tendency is now clear. It represents the basic guilt-feelings of Hermas (and his audience) over failure to live up to the fervent promise of Christian baptism. The world had been too close; and, in Hermas' own case, doubts about his own chastity and the fervor of his own household become the ultimate impulse in the construction of the series of disturbed, confusing dreams. Symbolically, the grandeur of the Tower, and the beauty and vitality of the healthy Vine and Willow Tree, represent the glory of the great co-operative work of building up the Church through the authentic Christianity of all its members. Psychologically the imagery thus lays the ground for the Second Repentance which, Hermas feels, the Church so needs. As an expression of Hermas' own personal problem, the erotic imagery which has been spiritually transformed suggests the resolution: Hermas will live in chastity with the Twelve Good Maidens; or, in the Pauline admonition (1 *Cor.* 7.29), those that have wives, shall be as if they had none. Thus the Woman who reminds him of his guilt becomes the Church renewed by penitence in pristine beauty; and it is with her, in a sense, that Hermas is to live in perfect chastity. There is a calm beauty in Hermas' symbolic Women, and it is this that makes his writing, for all its defects, unique in the early Church.

The seven epistles of St. Ignatius of Antioch form one of the most beautiful poetic treasures bequeathed by the second-century Church. In their Short Greek Version, the one which modern scholars now accept, they present a vivid, pathetic portrait of an aged though still vigorous Syriac bishop making his final triumphant journey across Asia "to fight with the beasts" of the Roman amphitheater. The date is late in the reign of the emperor Trajan, or early Hadrian.[14] Outside of Bithynia, martyrs were rare during these beneficent reigns, and the precise reasons which forced the bishop to go to Rome (he seems not to have been a Roman citizen) are unclear. In any case, from his native Antioch he proceeds by land stages and by sea to Cilicia, thence to the city of Philadelphia, to Sardis' ancient capital, and finally to Smyrna. At Smyrna, he tells us, Ignatius was received by Bishop Polycarp together with a number of ecclesiastical delegates from the communities of Ephesus, Tralles, and Magnesia. At Smyrna his scribe helps him write epistles to Ephesus, Tralles, Magnesia, and Rome. Finally from Smyrna he goes overland to the Troad, there to embark for Italy. Before leaving the coast he dispatched letters to Philadelphia, to Smyrna, and to his loyal friend, Polycarp. Written but a few weeks before his execution—the letter to the Romans is dated August 24, but the year is missing—the entire collection, with the curious covering letter of Polycarp to the Philippians, is

[14] On Ignatius, see Quasten, *Initiation* I.75 *ff*. See also Virginia Corwin, *St. Ignatius and Christianity in Antioch* (New Haven, 1960), with bibliography.

a mine of information on the structure and doctrine of the early Church.

In Ignatius' letters, Jesus and God are one, for Jesus is the Logos that breaks the ineffable Silence of the Godhead. For Ignatius, the mystical union with the Redeemer is achieved pre-eminently by the martyr's death, in becoming the pure bread of Christ, ground by the teeth of the beasts. Yet Ignatius' mysticism is firmly anchored in the hierarchic and sacramental structure of the Church. For the union of the triune Godhead, which is revealed in the Logos, is expressed outwardly in the unity of all those who have been baptized in Jesus and remain subject in love to their bishops, presbyters, and deacons (*Magn.* 6.1). This harmony of love is the mark of the true, "catholic" Church (*Smyrn.* 8.2), from which all heretical teachers have been "strained or filtered out" (*Phil.* 3.1) and excluded from the banquet of the *agape.* Union with Jesus, and therefore with the Godhead, is enjoyed only by those who eat "the suffering flesh" of the Saviour (*Smyrn.* 7.1), that "medicine of immortality" and "antidote against (the poison of) death" (*Ephes.* 20.2). It is within this harmony that the See of Rome, or "the Church which presides in Italy", is "pre-eminent in love" (*Rom.*, Introd.).

But the chief imagery for which the Ignatian corpus is most widely known deals with the glory of his approaching martyrdom. In the *Letter to the Trallians* (10) he calls martyrdom a fighting with the beasts, a gladiatorial combat. He urges Polycarp to be an athlete of God (*Polyc.* 2.3). Again, developing the Pauline armor-symbolism, he gives the traditional imagery a unique touch (*Polyc.* 6.2):

> Please the general in Whose ranks you serve and from Whom you must collect your pay. Let none of you turn deserter. It is baptism that is your armor, faith your helmet, love your spear, fortitude your panoply. And your good deeds will be deposits against all the back-pay that will be due you.

Using the Isaianic and Pauline imagery, Ignatius reveals his more intimate knowledge of the Roman legions; a system had been established by which part of the soldier's *stipendium* was deducted and not paid to him until the end of a campaign or of his term of enlistment. Indeed, Ignatius even uses, in the Greek text, the Latin words for the technical terms: *desertor,* deserter; *deposita,* deducted pay; *accepta,* back-pay. Finally, perhaps the most famous image of all is found in *Romans* 4.1; speaking of his coming martyrdom at Rome, he says:

> I am God's wheat, and I shall be ground by the teeth of the beasts, till I become the pure bread of Christ.

The beasts are the mill-stones which will separate the chaff from the crude grain. In *Ephesians* 20.2 he speaks of the Christians as breaking a bread, which is "the medicine of immortality, the antidote of death." Images from musical performances are suggested in *Philadelphians* 1.2: the bishop is a harp tuned to God's commandments; and there are references to a chorus or choir in *Ephesians* 19 and *Romans* 2.2. Again, there are two sets of coinages current in the world (*Magnesians* 5), bearing the die-stamp of God and that of the world. The heretics are like deadly herbs and poisonous fruit (*Trallians* 11); they are to be strained and filtered out of the good broth (*Philadelphians* 3.1); and evil teachers are like the tombs of the dead (*ibid.* 6.1), full of bones and corruption. Finally, Ignatius' elaborate allegories of the Christian life anticipate the writers of the late third and fourth century. Our quest for God is like the storm-tossed sailor seeking harbor or the harrassed pilot seeking a wind in a calm (*To Polycarp* 2.3). Or again, borrowing the building and temple metaphor from Paul, he develops it in *Ephesians* 9.1: we are all building stones prepared for the edifice of God; we are hoisted to position by the pulley of the Cross, and the rope is the Holy Spirit. We are fellow travellers on the road of life, clothed and adorned with the commandments, carrying with us the Lord, the Temple, and our own righteousness (*ibid.* 9.2).

Ignatius was a master of expression and at times rivals even St. Paul in richness and intensity. Some of Ignatius' imagery, as for example the pulley of the Cross, the military enlistment of Christianity, and the like, would favor a later date than is normally assigned to the letters; and the joyous picture of the martyr's death would perhaps suit a third century date. And yet the theology of the letters reflects the imagery of early Gnosticism and even Essenianism, and this would perhaps better fit the early second century. The doctrine and tone of the Ignatian epistles are all of a remarkable consistency, and the theory of a later forgery cannot be successfully supported.

We find a marked contrast as we turn to the writings associated with Polycarp. Polycarp's letter to the Philippians lacks coherence and unity; in part, at least, it purports to be a covering letter for the first collection of Ignatian epistles. Its austerity is relieved by the famous metaphor in which the consecrated widows of the Church are called an altar of God, smoking with burnt offerings. The reference is perhaps to the altar of incense in the Jewish Temple, and the image is found later in writers like Methodius and Gregory of Nyssa. The so-called *Martyrdom of Polycarp,* or the Letter to the Church of Philomelium from the community at Smyrna, has doubtlessly gone through several periods of editorial change, but preserves much earlier material. We find some striking symbolism connected with the martyr's death. Flames surround the body of Polycarp as though it were bread baked in an oven, or as if it were gold and silver in a furnace. Then, when (according to the account) they had to stab the saint in order to kill him, a dove emerged from the wound. It is an apocryphal incident due to a later hand: the bird represents the soul and perhaps, by suggestion, the Holy Spirit. That both blood and a dove emerged from the wound implies a reference to the Johannine symbolism of the blood and water that flowed from the side of Jesus on the Cross, and suggest the three that give testimony on earth in the Johannine epistle, blood, water and the Spirit.

The curious Alexandrian treatise called the *Epistle of Barnabas* comes from the reign of Trajan or Hadrian: it is a polemic against those who would hold a strict, literal interpretation of the Old Testament, and puts forward the Philonic or allegorical view in a way that reflects clear Alexandrian influence. There are two major images: that of the Jewish Temple, referring to the spiritual temple of the soul converted to the fervent Christian life; and the symbol of the Two Ways (18–19), which is briefly referred to in the *Didache* (1.1–2). The *Epistle of Barnabas* has an austerely unified tone and style, and reflects the hand of a single author; but its catechetical approach now seems to us lifeless and dull. There is, however, no evidence that the anonymous author made any pretence that his work was either apostolic or inspired.

The so-called *Epistle to Diognetus,* however, involves a number of interconnected problems: the question of the author and his purpose; and the problem of the unity of the work, and in particular the relevance of the appendix, § § 11–12. The first part (1–10) is quite confusing: the writer speaks of martyrs and persecution in a way that reminds one of the more violent days of the mid-third century (7.7 *f.*), he claims that Christians cannot be distinguished externally from the rest of mankind (not even in the matter of food and of chastity!)—a remark which, if taken seriously, would seem to reflect the first century of Christianity. Even Galen in the second century noticed the difference between Christians and pagans. All throughout, the author attempts to strike a primitive note: there is the war of the flesh against the spirit (6.5), and a portrait of the order of the world and the heavenly bodies (7.2), which recalls the argument for tranquillity used by Clement of Rome. The second part, on the other hand, would seem to come from a festal homily of the third century—perhaps for the Nativity or Baptism of the Lord (*cf.* 11.5). The style of this section is quite different from that of the first. The soul of the just is compared with a paradisial tree hanging with luscious fruit, untouched by the wiles of the serpent (12.1 *ff.*). Something odd has happened here, and I am sympathetic with those scholars who consider the epistle as a rhetorical fusion of at least two earlier works; to look for the redactor would hardly seem to be worth the effort.

The Symbolism of Martyrdom and Asceticism

CHAPTER FOUR

GIVEN THE outward circumstance of a law or ordinance against the Christians, it is easy to understand how the existing psychological resources would be mustered in support of those who were unjustly persecuted. In my monograph, *The Acts of the Pagan Martyrs,*[15] it was shown how death for an ideal had grown into an important behavior pattern from the earliest Greek literature down to the Stoics of the Roman empire. The very spread of martyr-literature became an incentive to further encouragement of resistance or rebellion against civil authority. For the Christian, however, in addition to the general philosophical principles of Socrates, there was the example of Christ himself. It is not the place here to discuss the legal basis of the persecutions. Even before the Decian law of the middle of the third century, which explicitly outlawed Christianity, there was adequate legal basis for proceeding against Christians whether as individuals or as a group. The Julian Law of *lèse-majesté,* on the one hand, gave the emperors and their magistrates pretty wide powers; and the ordinary police power of *coercitio* placed it within the competence of magistrates to suppress illegal gatherings, breaches of public order, and the like, especially when it was a question of the *humiliores* or the lower classes of the Roman social structure. Thus

[15] *The Acts of the Pagan Martyrs: Acta Alexandrinorum* (Oxford, 1954); and see also the discussion in *Theological Studies* 10 (1949), 555–64.

it was that the ultimate reasons for many of the trials and executions of the early martyrs have remained and will always remain obscure. On the one hand, there was adequate legal basis; on the other, it would appear, from the casual remarks of Tacitus, Pliny, and Marcus Aurelius, that many of the Christians sometimes went to the extent of provoking magistrates for one reason or another.

But if the martyr began early to identify himself with Christ before Pilate, we find also that the Roman magistrates are identified with the Adversary, the Evil One, Satan; and the mauling of the beasts in the amphitheatre culminates in the image of the Beast—especially in the *Epistle of the Churches of Lyons and Vienne,* describing the martyrdoms in France in the last quarter of the second century. The Latin *Acts of the Martyrs of Scilli,* on the other hand, from the same period, reflects the austerity of the Roman court record. It is important, however, in so far as it contains the first recorded Latin use of the word *martyr.* Even the *Apocalypse* (6.9) used the word *martyrion* for the "witness which they (the martyrs) gave." In its classic Greek usage, a martyr, in the rhetorical or legal sense, is one who gives evidence for the truth of something that he knows. Thus in the strict sense, the first martyrs were the apostles, since they bore testimony to the life and death of Christ. As the Fourth Gospel puts it, "and we know that his testimony is true" (*John* 21.24). In the sense used by the Christians from the days of the earliest persecutions, those who died for their faith were the supreme martyrs: for death would be the utmost proof of their conviction that Christ was God. Clement of Alexandria, however, in his *Miscellanies,* calls martyrdom "the perfect work of love," thereby stressing the more personal dimension of heroic death, inasmuch as it was evidence of the martyr's own love of Christ. Later on, Origen, too, stresses the personal element in martyrdom, and speaks of it as a kind of second baptism, a remission of sins, a sharing in the redemption of Christ for the sins of the world.

In Eusebius, that patient compiler of early documents, the martyr is *Christiphoros,* "the bearer of Christ." For Christ is in him, not only because, as in Paul and Ignatius of Antioch, he imitates the sufferings of Jesus, but also because his death is a witness to Christ's achievement. This is the predominant idea of the martyr in the early Church. It was the Alexandrian school that adapted this notion to catechetical teaching: the value of Jesus' Passion and death are more fully understood by reading the ordeals of the martyrs; these stand as proof of the Church's divine foundation. For Origen and Clement, however, the martyr's death becomes a personal apotheosis, in accordance with Jesus' words: Greater love than this . . . An act of perfect charity, death by martyrdom was the Christian's highest achievement, the standard against which all others were to be judged. It was precisely this line of thinking which prepared the way for the next great movement in the Church; the withdrawal to the desert, asceticism, monasticism. At any rate, so it continued for a century or more down to the Peace of the Church: accused of treason, public rioting, of meeting in clandestine fraternities, of refusing incense to the gods and the emperor's image, their forthright reply was always the testimony: "I am a Christian, a follower of Christus." Christians became the legal witnesses at the judgment which is passed on the Prince of Darkness by the Word of God as revealed in Jesus. Thus in all the changes which the word "martyr" was to undergo in the early Church, its connotation was always Johannine, and implied the intellectual conviction that Christ was the Messias sent by God to redeem the world, and that the Church of the faithful was his chosen representative on earth. Some writers, however, stress the more apologetic aspect of martyrdom, others the more personal.

Many of the symbols which were attached to martyrdom arose from the very nature of the Roman forms of death and torture. Crucifixion, burning alive, fighting with the beasts—the unholy trio of *crux, ignis, et bestiae,* the cross, fire, and beasts—were the usual forms of execution imposed on the *humiliores* or lower classes, (slaves, freedmen, and propertyless citizens) for the capital crimes. Thus the images taken from the gladiatorial games, fighting, wrestling, and so on; images of baking and burning, testing precious metals in the furnace, offering sacrifices on an altar (as in *Wisdom* 3.6). Still others were adapted from Paul and the *Apocalypse*: especially the battle images, the arming of the warrior, and the fight with the Beast of the Apocalypse.

One very curious document from the reign of Septimius Severus (about A.D. 202–3) is the *Passion of Saints Perpetua and Felicitas.*[16] All the available evidence would suggest that it is ultimately a Montanist document, originating in Africa perhaps from the circle of Tertullian himself. It is not only a *passio (martyrium),* an account of the actual sufferings of the martyrs; but it is also an apocalypse in its own right. If we may believe the anonymous author, chapters 3–10 (the account of Perpetua), and chapters 11–13 (the story of the martyr Satyrus), were taken from their own words; but the writer himself has supplied the framework contained in chapters 1–2, in which he points out the value of new visions and prophecies bestowed by the Holy Spirit for the building on the Church, and the conclusion, chapters 14 to the end.

The circumstances of the *Passion* are curious. Vibia Perpetua, a patrician lady from Thuburbo, south of the city of Carthage, is caught up in a persecution net which associated her with the holy catechist Satyrus, two young men named Saturninus and Secundulus, and the slaves Felicitas and Revocatus. Perhaps in the autumn of the year 202 the Christians were moved to a prison in Carthage, and here in dark dungeons they awaited their fate: to fight with beasts in the amphitheatre. Church officials obtained some measure of indulgence for the prisoners, and Perpetua was allowed to see her young baby as well as her aged father. The *Passion,* with its charming incident and pathos, is the archetype of all Christian martyr acts. But its uniqueness comes from the many visions the martyrs enjoyed before their death, told apparently in their own words. The vision of the catechist Satyrus (11–13) is perhaps the most stereotyped of them all: he sees the martyrs' bodies being borne towards the east by choirs of angels to the place where there is a white-haired man with a youthful face. There he sees a delightful garden, and a building whose walls were as of light, with a great throne for the young man surrounded by elders as in the book of the Apocalypse. Four angels lift the martyrs up to be kissed by the divine young man, and he gently strokes their faces as a choir intones, "Holy, holy, holy." Then all present exchange the liturgical kiss of peace.

[16] For the problems connected with the earliest martyr acts, see Quasten, *Initiation,* I.199 *ff.*, with the literature.

Satyrus suddenly awakes from his trance with the smell of a sweet incense in his nostrils.

The incidents surrounding Perpetua and Felicitas form the major part of the *Passion.* The author delicately portrays the two young women, Perpetua who had given birth before imprisonment, the slave Felicitas imprisoned with her now eight months' pregnant. There is a deeper symbolism here, which is developed when the jailer mocks the young girl in her labor pains: "What will you do when you face the lions?" But Felicitas replies: "Now it is I who suffer; there in the arena someone else will be within me." The constant imagery throughout the *Passion* of childbearing, nursing, the drinking of milk, and so on, precisely fit the author's intention. For he is not only interested in the warmth and charm of these courageous Christian women, but he is suggesting a comparison with the Woman of the Apocalypse who gives birth to her child under the threat of the Dragon.

The sequence of Perpetua's visions is much more mysterious (cc. 3–10). In the first one she sees a very tall bronze ladder rising to the sky, recalling perhaps the one that Jacob saw. To its sides are attached instruments of torture and execution, suggesting the various forms of martyrdom. The people climbing it bear the marks of their execution. Satyrus reaches the top first and cries to Perpetua below. At the foot of the ladder is a monstrous dragon, but Perpetua crushes him beneath her sandal as she climbs to the top. It is reminiscent of Iahweh's promise to the woman of *Genesis* 3:15. Then, at the top, there is a vast garden full of light, with a man in white hair dressed as a shepherd, milking sheep. He looks at her lovingly. It is the Good Shepherd, and he gives Perpetua milk to drink with joined hands (the Eucharist), while all around say "Amen." The milk imagery is most apt at this point, and perhaps anticipates the symbols we find in Methodius later on: Mother Church who feeds her children with the milk of immortality.

Visions two and three are of less interest: they concern Perpetua's deceased brother Dinocrates attempting to drink from a font that is too high for him. The visions reflect perhaps the mediumistic phenomena that were current in the Montanistic church at the time. In Perpetua's fourth Vision she is changed to a man, stripped and rubbed with oil, and pitted against an Egyptian boxer. The boxer tries to trip her by getting hold of her feet, but Perpetua treads on his face and later throws him to the ground, defeating him. For the reader, however, the symbolism becomes clear: it is the Beast once again, on whose head Perpetua trod as she climbed the ladder to Paradise.

The *Passion* for all its undoubted charm is a fantastic, emotionally charged work; and its slight tinge of eroticism recalls the imagery of *The Shepherd* of Hermas. It is far from being, as some have called it, the most charming document of the early Church. In addition, it reveals the fine Italian hand of Tertullian, even if he is not responsible for its complete form.

With works like the Ignatian corpus, the *Martyrdom of Polycarp*, the *Letter of the Churches of Lyons and Vienne*, the Montanist *Passion*, and some of the *Acta martyrum* which closely follow the Roman court records, the symbolism of Christian martyrdom was established for many centuries to come. At a very early date the martyr acts began to become edifying fiction, catechesis, or apology. Sometimes what were bare court records were filled out with more interesting details; sometimes the entire account—as the *Passion of St. Cecilia*—would be completely invented. In the transition from the authentic to the partly or wholly fictional *Acta*, six principles seem to have been operative: 1) dramatic interest, such that the exchanges between the magistrate and the martyrs would be made more striking; 2) the *horror vacui*, or desire to fill in gaps in the story; 3) edification and instruction, so that certain doctrines or lessons could be taught by suggestions; 4) etiology, or an attempt to explain the existence of local feasts or cults; 5) imitation, or borrowing from other sources; 6) emulation, that the local martyr should not be surpassed in any way by one venerated elsewhere.

What makes the problem doubly complicated is the fact that a good number of our extant martyr acts come down to us through official channels, such as the edition made by Eusebius of Caesarea (referred to in his *History of the Church*) and entitled *On the Ancient Martyrs*, published about the year A.D. 300. In it were the story of the martyrs of Vienne and Lyons; the so-called *Acts of Apollonius*, assigned to the reign of Commodus but perhaps not entirely authentic; and an account of the martyrs at Alexandria under Decius. It does not seem to have included the martyrs of Scilli and the *Passion of Perpetua and Felicitas.* At any rate, it is easy to see how it could happen that many of the details of actual trials, once set down for the record, would now be recast on the more symbolic level of apology and instruction for the sake of the catechumenate. As Tertullian had said: the blood of martyrs was the seed of Christians. In the *Passion of Perpetua and Felicitas* the martyr would be the perfect Christian, blessed with an apocalyptic vision of Paradise. Soon the testimony of martyrdom would shift and a new expression of the concept of witness would emerge. This would be the "martyr in conscience," who died daily in the struggle against the flesh—the ascetic and the monk.

It was around the middle of the third century, about the time of the persecution of the emperor Decius, that a new psychological awareness of the implications of the Gospel developed. The ascetics and anchorites, whose intellectual center was Alexandria, gave a far more intense, austere interpretation of the words of Jesus. As early as 162 the pagan doctor Galen, who openly disliked the Christians, had yet to praise them for what he thought was an extraordinary practice of chastity over long periods of time. Then, in the first quarter of the third century, we have, through the not always trustworthy account of Eusebius, the story of Origen, fasting and going without sleep in order to give more time to the Scriptures. Even Gregory Thaumaturgus, who was a student of Origen's, tells us of the remarkable impression which his master's piety made on him. There is, in his *Panegyric on Origen,* little evidence of the mysticism and austerity that Eusebius makes so much of; but it is clear that Gregory thought him to be the greatest scholar and theologian of the Christian world.

It is hard to be certain whether Origen's doctrine or his personal influence had the greatest effect on the growth of the ascetical movement. It was, in any case, a combination of both. Origen had, from his youth, been a catechist at the Alexandrian school. His father, Leonides, had died a martyr under Septimius Severus; and Origen himself was to be severely tortured during the investigations carried out by Decius. His unbalanced temperament led him to self-mutilation in literal obedience to the Gospel parable; and his bishop Demetrius refused to ordain him, though he was sufficiently aware of his talent to leave him at the head of the Alexandrian school. It was Origen's unique genius to discover that the heart of any Christian catechesis must be a thorough study of the Scriptures. To this end he studied Hebrew and the commentaries of Philo, and compared the various Greek versions of the Old Testament. A remarkable pedant, an eclectic philosopher of wide background, if he was also an ascetic, it was, one feels, only subordinate to his main purpose. Indeed, his writings suggest his own terrible struggles and reflect an austerity that is quite unusual at this early period. We read, for example, in one of his *Homilies on Jeremias*:[17]

> There are some who choose not to exercise the faculty of marriage, but to humble themselves and to suffer, to chastise the body with fasting, to bring it into subjection by certain types of abstinence, and indeed completely to mortify the deeds of the flesh by the spirit.

Eusebius, in the miniature biography of Origen in the sixth book of the *Ecclesiastical History,* has surely exaggerated the asceticism of Origen; but it cannot be denied that his vivid portrait had, in its turn, a profound influence upon the developing monastic movement.

The emerging pattern becomes clearer when we consider the testimony of Dionysius, Bishop of Alexandria, preserved in Eusebius' sixth book. Dionysius tells of the many pious Christians who tried to evade the Decian inquisition by running off to the caves and the oases of the Nile Valley. Here had been the regular hiding places for condemned prisoners, tax delinquents, and the like, under the Roman administration. It would be the normal spot for a retreat during the time of persecution. The Nile Valley, too, had been known for its communities of dedicated pagan

[17] For a discussion of Origen's influence on early Christian asceticism, see my monograph, *The Problem of Ascetical Fasting in the Greek Patristic Writers,* in *Traditio* 12 (1956), 1–64, esp. 6, 38, and *passim.* Cf. also H. von Camphenhausen, *The Fathers of the Greek Church* (tr. by S. Godman, New York, 1959), pp. 40–56, on Origen's achievement.

priests and priestesses, and also for the colonies of ascetic Jewish students of the Torah who seem to have resembled the Covenanters of the Dead Sea. In some such concrete context as this are we probably to imagine the origins of the anchoretic movement: the desert with its calm, the influence of both pagan and Jewish groups who had gone there either to study or pray, the numbers of timid Christians who feared their faith might not be strong enough to withstand the inquisition and torture of the Roman soldiery—all of this with a disgust for the world of cruelty and lust in which they lived and the expectation that retreat (*anachoresis* is the Greek word) would solve the problem. It was to this new psychological milieu that the older symbols of battle, struggle, and the apocalypse, would be applied; and a good many others would be added.

It was about the year 270 that we first hear of definite individuals going into the Egyptian desert for ascetical reasons. The first historical figure seems to have been St. Antony, whom we know chiefly through the life attributed to Athanasius. St. Jerome, in an attempt to put someone in the desert even before Antony, invented Paul, the First Hermit; but the life that Jerome circulated was denounced even in his lifetime, and there seems to be no historical foundation for Paul—save, of course, in the numberless anonymous and forgotten men and women who wandered off to the desert during the days of Decius.

It was the *Life of Antony* that had the most widespread influence on the growth of monasticism both in the East and the West. Antony went out alone into the desert about twenty years after the Decian persecution; and within fifteen years he was surrounded by monks or anchoretes who lived in huts nearby in order to imitate his example and be guided by his wisdom and advice. Here at its core was the origin of the religious life: poverty grew out of the very nature of their desert existence; chastity out of their solitary life of meditation; obedience out of their desire to be guided by one who was older, wiser, holier. *The Life of Antony*[18] was composed at Alexandria about the year 356–7 during the Arian persecutions; it was written under the influence

[18] See Robert T. Meyer, *St. Athanasius: The Life of Saint Antony* (Ancient Christian Writers 10, Westminster, Md., 1950).

of Bishop Athanasius, who had always encouraged monastic spirituality among his dependents and had himself retreated to the desert during one of his frequent exiles from the city. His own career, and his travels, especially to the West in quest of vindication, helped to disseminate the Antonian ideal; and about the year 361 it was translated into Latin. It was in its Latin version that it had such a deep influence upon the growing ascetical movement in Italy and France. Origen's life and writings together with the *Life of Antony* perhaps did more to establish the ascetic pattern of behavior than anything else in the history of primitive Christianity.

The *Life* purports to have been written by Athanasius himself and, in form, is a letter to monks outside of Egypt who have asked for information on Antony's way of life (*Preface*); the seal of authenticity is Antony's gift of some old sheepskins "one to Athanasius and the other to Serapion" (§91). Within the framework of Antony's frightfully austere life among the tombs and desert places along the Nile, his simple courage during persecution, his struggling with diabolical obsession, is set the most important part of the book, the discourse on ascetical perfection (§ § 16–43). Typical of many of the earlier treatments of the subject, there are two parts: (1) that ascetical perfection is within our power by a "daily dying to self"; and (2) that we must learn to deal with the attacks of the demons. The preoccupation with demonology strikes the modern reader as strange; one is tempted to believe that either this developed from an exaggerated view of body needs and drives, especially as they became more clamorous under the overseverity of desert existence, or else that some of the early anchorites were subject to psychotic seizures or forms of epilepsy. In the *Life of Antony*, however, it may be that some of the stories of daemonic obsession are inventions of the pious author. In the end, of course, the unlearned Antony delivers a stern attack on the Arian heretics (§ § 69–70). Here, if anywhere, is the mark of Athanasian influence.

The picture of the holy man in the desert, surrounded by demons, struggling with his own temptations, and thereby gaining strength beyond anything the flesh could achieve, was to become an important ascetic symbol for later ages. In addition, with the shift of the martyr-image to the life of asceticism, and the adaptation of some of the Neo-Platonic symbols, the monk would be fully armed with a psychological support for his life of austerity.

Athanasius, if he was the author of the *Life of Antony*, surely based his account on what he had heard from the Egyptian monks who were his intimates. But most important for our purpose is § 47: "When the persecution had ended . . . Antony went back to his solitary hut, and there became a daily martyr in conscience, constantly fighting the battle of the faith." And this is explained by saying that he constantly fasted, wore haircloth, never bathed, or used oil. But how could this be considered a martyrdom? In the original sense of the word, Antony was testifying to the Atonement of Christ in his flesh; he was witness to the truth (as Clement of Alexandria defined martyrdom) that "greater love than this no man has, than he lay down his life for his friend." By a living metaphor, Antony was by inflicting pain on himself, dying daily.

It was a curiously rude and sometimes morbid asceticism that emerged from Antonian spirituality, which later developed into obvious excess with the rise of the Fathers of the Desert. Even if we cannot believe all the tales told by Pachomius or the collection *The Sayings of the Fathers*, it is clear that the concept of martyrdom by self-inflicted pain had become extreme and excessive. But meanwhile a more moderate monasticism developed in the area of Lycia about the year 290, as we find it reflected in the work of Methodius of Olympus, especially his *Symposium on Chastity*. He stresses, above all, the quiet life of the community, celibacy, meditation on the doctrines of the Church and on the mystical meaning of the Scriptures. The women he directed seem to have dressed modestly; he stressed the virtues, and urged no external practices save the avoidance of strong drink. There is no mention of any external discipline save that of the liturgical fast of Holy Week. Of his ascetical-mystical doctrine we shall have more to say farther on. But it is important to realize that his more moderate spirituality co-existed with the austerities of the Alexandrian and Egyptian ascetics.

Throughout all of the ascetical writers, the lives of Pachomius, the eulogies of the Fathers found in the homilies of Chrysostom, the later monastic directors like Abbot Nilus, John Climacus, and the rest, the most pervasive image is that of the Battle, the fight against the powers of darkness, and the passions of men which they seem to employ for the destruction of the good. Just as the symbol of the *martyr* or witness passed from actual martyrdom to that of the "martyr in conscience" in Athanasius and Methodius, so now the persecution of the ascetic—once the Peace of the Church was achieved—is accomplished within his own soul. As the Abbot Nilus put it: "Persecution is present . . . in anger, in wicked desires, in grief, fear, envy, gluttony and drunkenness, and in all other motions which disturb the soul" (*Epistle* 3). Our martyrdom, says Chrysostom, is to endure the sufferings of the world. To fight well, says the writer called Pseudo-Macarius, we must constantly have the ideal of death for Christ's sake before our minds.

Thus the Pauline and Apocalyptic battle imagery dominated the monastic literature. Then, with the spread of the *Life of Antony* and the lives of Pachomius, the battle lines became more clearly drawn. The great Adversary who had introduced evil into the world by seducing Adam was bent on the destruction of every human soul. For some of the writers he is pictured as assigning an individual demon to each soul, to discover his weakest point of entry. In others, hordes of demons enter into a man when he allows himself to experience any pleasure: sleep, food, marriage. Their motive is jealousy for man, or simple malice, or hatred of Christ. In the *Sayings of the Fathers* we hear of an organized army of fiends who tempt men by a fixed routine: from gluttony, to lust, and so on to the other capital sins. In writers like the Semi-Arian Basil of Ancyra the very position of the bodily organs and the effects of certain foods is used to confirm the relationship between the demons and the sinful inclinations of the body. The pseudo-scientific synthesis of Evagrius of Pontus tended to confirm this symbolism from an ascetico-dogmatic point of view. It was Evagrius[19] who devised the classification of the seven deadly

[19] On Evagrius of Pontus (346–399), see the summary article and bibliography by K. Baus, *Lexikon für Theologie und Kirche*, III, 1140 *f.; cf.* also O. Chadwick, *John Cassian: A Study in Primitive Monasticism* (Cambridge University Press, 1950), pp. 82 *ff.*, 94 *ff.*, and *passim*, with the bibliography quoted.

sins; and in his writing the entire ascetical process becomes systematized for the first time. After uprooting the seven (or really eight) deadly sins, the soul must be deprived so far as possible of its passions, and then of its very thoughts and images; only then can it be filled with the notion and love of God Triune, shining within it like a sparkling sapphire. Thus the soul rises, as on a Platonic ladder, to a special intuitive union with God.

The "stripping of the soul," which we find germinally in Origen, now becomes an accepted process, and, as we shall see, the ascetical writers would begin to support it with a special sequence of images: battle, struggle, athletic contests, training. For the wrestling with the powers and principalities, with the Devil and his minions, could only be prepared for by a long period of training or *askêsis.* Just as the gladiator's body could be brought to a peak of physical condition in order to endure prolonged labor and hardship with apparent ease, so too, it was felt, the soul and the faculties could be "trained" by the doctrines of the Church, by the Scriptures, and by the traditional ascetical principles of the Fathers of the Desert.

Closely allied with this there grew up the concept of holy emulation, that many writers, like M. Viller, P. de Ghellinck, and others, have discussed in their treatment of the asceticism of the first centuries. Competition was extreme to see who could fast the longest, the most rigorously, and live in the most painful way. Further, the results of this suppression of body needs was supposed to produce a certain release of the soul, a clarifying of the mind's vision, and a preparation for the intuition of God even in this life. In some writers there is the suggestion that prolonged *askêsis* could succeed in suppressing all bodily inclinations whatsoever, so as to reproduce in some sense, the condition of Adam and Eve in Paradise.

One final example we may take from a most extraordinary phase of Christian austerity: the period of the Syrian stylites. These rigorous ascetics who lived on tall pillars, about the fifth and sixth centuries of our era, represent perhaps for us today the ultimate folly of primitive asceticism. The Abbé Duchesne in his *History of the Church* (1912) found it shocking that ecclesiastical authorities did not put a stop to the stylite movement. But he thus reveals a misunderstanding of the psychology and religious symbolism of the period. The movement of the stylites was, in a sense, the logical culmination of the philosophy of self-immolation and removal from material things that began with Origen, Eustathius, and the Neo-Platonists. The more one could raise oneself from matter, so much the more might one release the forces of the spirit. Simeon Stylites the Elder began a great wave of pillar-sitting when he first climbed a pillar and remained there until his death in the latter part of the fifth century. He is by no means a legendary figure: the Bollandists, who are not wont to deal lightly with miraculous tales, are forced to admit that the basic facts of his life have been authenticated.

It is an odd fact that the majority of the early stylite ascetics were Syrians; and it may be that Lucian, the pagan satirist who often touched the fringes of Christianity, offers a clue to the practice. He describes, in *The Syrian Goddess,* how pillar-climbers used to climb up and live on two columns that were placed before the Temple of the god Dionysus in Hierapolis. It was, he suggests, an elevation of man closer to the gods; and the pillar-climbers were apparently expected to pray for the welfare of the city. In any case, we know that the elder Simeon had been a poor, simple Syrian shepherd, who entered a monastery near Antioch but was expelled apparently for practicing excessive austerities. Indeed, his attempt to pass the rest of his life chained to a rock had been foiled by ecclesiastical authorities. Somewhere, somehow, he conceived the idea of living atop a column. It was about the year 425. He moved to the village of Telnesin, not far from Antioch, and there, on the pretext of avoiding the importunities of the curious crowds, he erected a pillar which, in its last phase, seems to have reached a height of over thirty-six feet. At the top was a kind of fence; and a crude rope ladder led to the top so that the monk could receive his meagre ration of food and water. Occasionally he would send down messages to the people below; he prayed; he sometimes preached. He perhaps often applied to himself the words of the Gospel of John: If I be lifted up, I will draw all things to me. And this was the life he led, if we are to believe the substantially trustworthy Greek and Syriac sources, for over thirty years until his death, Sept. 2, A.D. 459.

But the end was not yet. As with every movement there were

a number of imitators and emulators. As the shrewd Père de Ghellinck once remarked, one gets the impression that some of the early ascetics acted as though there were some spiritual record which had to be bettered. But it is not our purpose to trace the entire history of the stylite movement as it spread down to the tenth century, and even later, through Egypt, Mesopotamia, and Greece. One early imitator of Simeon is known to us in the West from Gregory of Tours' *History of the Franks:* the curious monk and deacon Vufolaic, or St. Walafroy as he is more popularly known in France. His story illustrates better than anything else the change of ideas that took place when asceticism was transferred to the West in the works of Athanasius and Cassian. In his cordial, chatty way, Gregory of Tours tells us that he met the monk Vufolaic about the year 585 near the town of Yvois in the territory of Trèves, and got the story from his own mouth (*History* 8.15). As part of the monk's campaign against the worship of Diana in the area and other pagan practices, he set up a column on a hill, from which he used to preach to the local people, inveighing against their stubbornness in worshipping a pagan goddess. The rude diet and damp, cold winters soon made him ill, his body covered with sores. Now at last he discovered the difference between France and the mild climate of the Egyptian desert:

> When winter came [he tells Gregory] I was stiff with the cold, and the terrible frost made the nails drop from my toes, while icicles hung from my beard like the melted wax on candles. The district, you see, had a reputation for its many hard winters.

He persevered nonetheless. The statues were destroyed; his body sores and pustules were healed by the application of some holy chrism from the shrine of St. Martin of Tours. Then, when he still remained on his column, a delegation of French bishops came and gathered below. They shouted up to the holy man above:

> The way you follow is not the right way. Don't think that an obscure person like you can imitate Simeon the stylite of Antioch. The air of this place will not allow you to endure this torture.

The good monk then came down at their bidding, hoping to get back to his column on another day. But one of the bishops, he tells us, "invited him out to see an estate some distance away." And when Vufolaic returned to his hill on the following day, he realized that the bishop had sent workmen with crowbars and axes to shatter his precious pillar. "I wept very much," he said. But surely he could not disobey the injunction of the bishops. "So now I have to be content with life in the community," he concluded lamely. And so Gregory ended the story. It is a vivid account, and from it we can see how divergent were the ways of East and West. At any rate, it is clear that the stylite movement could have but a short life in France. From Simeon to Vufolaic, it was surely an incredible chapter in the history of Christian piety.

Two Greek Fathers were especially successful in exploiting the symbols of monasticism within the context of their daily preaching: Gregory of Nazianzus and John Chrysostom. For both—for Gregory in his poetry, and Chrysostom in his prose—the monastic movement became the embodiment of the perfect fulfillment of the mandate of Christ to the Church. Gregory Nazianzen's poetry, with all its massive bulk, is a good example of diligence without inspiration. As he explains in the poem which is entitled *On My Poetry* (II.1, poem number 39, in the Benedictine edition), "if pagan poets perhaps surpass us in style and expression, we remain far superior to them in contemplation (*theoria*)." And of Gregory, this is eminently true: his pieces are metrically correct, but dull. Even the occasion of an epithalamium on the wedding of the pious virgin Olympias, later deaconess of Constantinople and spiritual protegé of Chrysostom, fails to raise him to any Pindaric heights. He can only repeat the boring commonplaces of Christian asceticism on the eve of her new life. It is her inner beauty that is most important; she must avoid sensuality in dress, in thought, in action; she must be subject to her husband in all things, yet try to persuade him not to be absorbed in sexual pleasure on holy days (*Poems* II.2.6).

Perhaps the best of his pieces are the dramatic dialogues between the flesh and the spirit, between the monk and his lower inclinations. These sections seem to be based on Cynic prototypes. For example, in a long piece entitled *"Four-Line Sayings"* (I.2.33), we have the dialogue, lines 73–6:

> "An alms," says my belly.
> If you'd be temperate, I'd be glad to.
> But if you yield to lower passion,
> It's offal you'll get, and little of that.

Again in *An Anacreontic to Himself* (II.1.88) we find the dilemma in vivid colors (lines 87–92):

> So this is what you want: the plucking of strings,
> The clapping of hands, the arousal of lust,
> The sensuous motions of dancing boys
> And the dances of girls indecently garbed?
> Are you hungry? Well, there's bread and meal,
> If you want it, and salt for your seasoning.

It is a cruel, unnatural dichotomy that Gregory paints. Perhaps his most striking poem on this theme is the famous one, *The Debate between the World and the Spirit,* found in the theological collection (I.2.8). Kosmos, the World, and Pneuma, the Spirit, go before the Byzantine magistrate to obtain a settlement in a lawsuit: he is to decide which has the superior way of life in very much the same way as he would settle a property dispute according to the Roman Code. At one point the litigants forget the judge and the dispute becomes quite excited (lines 91–104):

THE WORLD: But I love pleasure.

THE SPIRIT: And my pleasure is to have no pleasure. I do not want my body swollen with food, overwhelmed with the diseases of the rich, belching from my throat the sickly sweet odor of filth, weighing down my spirit with a mass of fat.

THE WORLD: I love sweetmeats!

THE SPIRIT: Bread is my food, and plain water my drink surpassing sweet, and salt my only seasoning.

THE WORLD: I love the fragrance of perfume, I love singing and the beating of feet, the clapping of hands and moving to rhythm. I love the symphony of musical instruments.

THE SPIRIT: Yes, indeed. . . . But our psalmody is far superior to all your musical compositions.

When the bewildered magistrate is finally asked for his decision, he cannot pronounce one. By a final irony, he insists that both parties must practice coexistence, with the World obedient and submissive to the Spirit. The conclusion suggests a mock-divorce proceeding, in which the plea for separation *a mensa et toro* is unsuccessful. For all his Stoic-Cynic exaggeration, Gregory saw that the spirit and the flesh must somehow find a *modus vivendi* and compromise their differences in this life. How this is to be achieved, however, he does not say.

In the light of his views of the ascetic life, it is all the more surprising to find in his *Eulogy of Virginity* (*Poems* I.2.1) a long section on the praises of married life. The hymn to God's plan for the generation of the human race (lines 28–261) strikes a strangely discordant note; but it was intended to mark a contrast with the far greater pleasures of the life dedicated to virginity and seclusion. Nonetheless, Gregory's praise of the married state is unique among the Greek Fathers of the Church:

> Great is the value of a good marriage to man!
> It was marriage that taught men wisdom, and probed the
> deep,
> Searched all that is bound by the earth, the seas,
> The heavens. Marriage founded city laws, and early
> Founded cities. Marriage by man's cunning
> Created all the arts, filled the marketplace,
> The homes, the gymnasia. It gave us armies
> In war; filled tables at symposia, gave us the chorus
> Which hymned the gods before the smoking altar.

The eulogy goes on for many more lines, and it self-consciously concludes:

> This then is marriage. And yet there is a higher state
> Far, far superior.

But such praise, grudging though it is, is a precious testimony to Gregory's humanity.

One of the Greek Fathers who most successfully transformed the symbols of monasticism was St. John Chrysostom. Many of his descriptions of the life of the consecrated men and women of the desert are even more poetic than the verses of Nazianzen. As a monk Chrysostom had not strayed far from his native Antioch; but he had read of the Egyptian deserts, and had at least heard of the miraculous life of Antony, the first hermit. In one of his homilies on Matthew (*hom.* 8.5), commenting on the Angel's message to the Holy Family, "Fly into Egypt," he embarks on one of his favorite digressions: the unbelievable austerities of the men and women of the Egyptian desert:

> They have put off all things, and are totally crucified to the world. . . . But not simply because they fast and watch do they feel justified in staying idle all the day. After giving the night to sacred hymns and to vigils, they devote their day to prayer and to manual labor in imitation of the Apostle.

Indeed, arising from his nostalgia for the ascetic communities which lived outside Antioch, and to which he once belonged, there is a subtle antinomy throughout Chrysostom's works: the opposition of the Desert and the City, which reminds us almost of Augustine's City of God and City of Earth. In the Desert is the hope of Christianity, the source of spiritual strength and insight into the meaning of life. In his treatise *Against Those Who Oppose the Monastic Life* he defends the monks of Antioch against those who accused them of corrupting the young; rather, Chrysostom pleads, all good Christians should want their sons trained to goodness and purity in the *asceteria* outside the city. If a torch, he says, were laid to a house for the purpose of robbing it, no one would blame the men who led the inmates out to safety; if a city were being persecuted by a tyrant, they would be praised who led the citizens out until reinforcements came. So is it with the sinful cities of the world, especially Antioch; and the monks are merely leading the way to salvation (*Against Those Who Oppose* I.7). In times of plague and epidemic we lead our children out of the city to a place of safety (*ibid.* III.6); the good monk tries to rescue men from shipwreck on the sea (I.7), but once safely in port, he can only look out sadly and watch the destruction of so many mortals (III.11); there he sees ships sinking and dashed to pieces, with men in agony clinging vainly to spars (*To the Fallen Monk Theodore* 2.5).

In his early essay, *The Comparison Between the Monk and the*

King, he sharply contrasts the two domains which monk and ruler control; the ruler his city, the monk his passions. Again there is the polarity between City and Desert. The ascetic conquers heretics and demons, spends his night praising God, anticipates the song of the birds, lives alone in chastity and austerity. The king spends the day with his officers, who are given to lust and drinking, snores through a heavy sleep after a riotous banquet. The monk dies like a martyr; the king ultimately falls on the sword of his rival. For the monk, however, the Cross is his sword by which he cuts through the lines of his enemies.

Another sequence of connected images can be found in Chrysostom's discussion of the education of children, especially in the two treatises *Against Those Who Oppose the Monastic Life* and *On Pride and the Education of Children.* Children are like waxen images to be moulded; statues to be carved by craftsmen; portraits to be painted slowly by the hands of devoted artists, growing by gentle accretions of pigment (*Against Those Who Oppose* III.12). Or again the soul of the child is like a walled city to be ruled by a good king: the walls are the bodily faculties, the gates are the five senses. The citizens—following the analogy drawn in Plato's *Republic*—are the three spiritual faculties, the Understanding, the Irascible, and Desire (*epithymia*); and they dwell in three areas, the brain, the heart, and the liver. The good teacher must act like a city-planner who wishes to construct a most efficient and happy city. But, Chrysostom suggests, the city is also filled with a number of criminals and degenerate men who must be restrained by force or even expelled as undesirable aliens if the city is to be under the secure rule of law. This comparison is chiefly developed in *On Pride and the Education of Children,* a treatise that is unique in the history of Christian pedagogy. But, as he develops his ideas in the companion book *Against Those Who Oppose,* the only place where the ideal education can be imparted is within the austere hermitages outside the city of Antioch.

City and Desert, the Flesh and the Spirit—between these there is a constant warfare, in which, unlike worldly wars, there is never a time for sleeping, never a truce. Indeed, it is with the monastic ideal in mind that Chrysostom constantly inveighs against the luxuries of the city, against pleasure, the games, marriage, music, drama, banquets, the seductive makeup of women. Unintentionally amusing is his picture, in the homilies on Matthew (30.6), of women with makeup:

> like bears with bloody mouths, with eyebrows blackened as though from the soot of a kitchen pot, their cheeks whitened like the wall of sepulchres.

Quite shocking to us today is Chrysostom's portrait of female beauty in his letter *To the Fallen Monk Theodore.* Theodore had abandoned the desert for the charms of a woman he once loved named Hermione. Chrysostom therefore uses all the resources of his rhetoric to inspire the fallen monk with disgust and to detach him from the unfortunate woman. Thus Chrysostom analyzes Hermione's charms with the cold detachment of a primitive surgeon (I.14):

> The whole of her bodily beauty is nothing less than phlegm, blood, bile, rheum, and the fluid of digested food. . . . If you consider what is stored up behind those lovely eyes, the angle of the nose, the mouth and cheeks, you will agree that the well-proportioned body is merely a whitened sepulchre.

If once the flesh ceases to be bathed in the body's humors, it begins to corrupt in disgusting fashion; indeed, the bodily effluvia only prove what a repulsive vessel it is:

> When you see a cloth with anything on it like phlegm or spittle, you cannot even touch it with your fingertips or look at it. How then can you become enamored of the storehouse and repository of all these things?

Here, we can see, was the area of Chrysostom's rhetorical mastery—and not in the realm of dogmatic development. In one very striking image a woman's face becomes the symbol for all that is passing and trivial in this world; in his first *Sermon on Eutropius* (I.3), Chrysostom teaches his audience that in the fall of the eunuch Eutropius they can now see the meaning of human life:

> Young girls have left their chambers, and matrons their rooms, their men have left the marketplace—all of you

> have rushed here to see human nature laid bare, to see the swift mutability of all things: for here you see the harlot's face of yesterday (for it was a borrowed, meretricious beauty) washed clean as though by a sponge of all its makeup and artifice, revealing the truth as more ugly than a wrinkled old hag.

It is clear that Chrysostom's power lay within the limited area of the ascetic and moral; but it is here especially where his imagination soared to great heights of symbolism. Literal and austere in his commentary on the Scriptures, he reveals supreme poetic power in the domain he most loved to preach on: the City and the Desert, the interior warfare set up by the very conditions of Christ's demand for moral perfection. Chrysostom's vivid portrait of this clash remains quite unique till the rise of the reform movements of the Middle Ages.

The Divine Image in Man and the Mystical Ascent of the Soul

CHAPTER FIVE

ONE OF the most dramatic images of the early Fathers was derived from the Priestly Tradition which was at the basis of *Genesis* 1.26, in which man is called the image (*tselem*) and likeness (*demût*) of the Lord.[20] Most likely these words are intended in the text as practical synonyms: man's resemblance to Iahweh is based on his intelligence and on his superiority over all creation. It would seem in any case that most of the Fathers did not distinguish between image and likeness. For those who did, it is an easy matter to explain the catastrophic effects of man's primaeval Fall: Adam lost the likeness, but retained the image, his basic resemblance to God. For most, however, who identify image and likeness, such as Cyril of Alexandria,

[20] For a discussion of the doctrine of the divine image in man, see Gerhart B. Ladner, *The Idea of Reform: Its Impact on Christian Thought and Action in the Age of the Fathers* (Cambridge, Mass., 1959), esp. pp. 83–107, with the full bibliography given there. Ladner rightly sees the concept of God's image as an important influence on the reform movement throughout the patristic period. For some of the crucial metaphors associated with the doctrine, see especially pp. 92–4. *Cf.* also W. J. Burghardt, *The Image of God in Man According to Cyril of Alexandria* (Catholic University Studies in Christian Antiquity 14, Washington, D.C., 1957).

Methodius, and (with distinctions) Gregory of Nyssa, man's resemblance to God is developed by a series of analogies drawn from sculpture and painting. In the most common of metaphors, the Fathers portray the divine image in man as obscured by mud, grime, and smoke; or, again, as a painting ruined by the application of the wrong colors. On seeing the divine traits, as Methodius tells us, in Christ, as in an icon, man is able to restore the image of God within himself. The overpainting in the course of time has been the various vices; now the practice of the virtues will bring back the true coloring.

Again, for Gregory of Nyssa the work of Christian perfection is like the carving of a statue: only by long, painful chiselling and polishing can the true image, in accordance with the divine Craftsman's idea, perfectly emerge. Methodius seems more familiar with the image of casting statues in bronze or baking clay in a mould. Indeed, the whole history of salvation is summed up in the image of the divine Potter creating vessels for His glory; the same clay that produced Adam's body, dissolved into earth, was remoistened and recast in the mould of the Virgin's womb as a new vessel of election. In a similar way, the divine Craftsman moulds men within the womb; born, however, without Adam's original innocence, the clay of men's bodies is more prone to corruption and decay, and the senses are more easily confused by the waves of worldly and sinful impressions which dash upon them from the outside. The casting of Adam within the mould of the earth, Christ's body within the womb of Mary, and men today within their mother's womb—all these are parallel with the gestation and birth of the Christian from the womb of the Virgin Mother, the Church. The image of the divine Potter, borrowed from Isaias and St. Paul, is not yet, in the early Fathers, a symbol for the problem of God's foreknowledge and predestination, as it was later to be for the theologians of the Middle Ages and the Renascence. But from the imagery of statue and icon we have moved into the metaphor of birth and procreation. Christians are born from Mother Church and resemble Christ because they were conceived in her during the glorious ecstasy of the Passion. The fecundity of the Church comes from Christ, as did Eve's from Adam; and so her sons resemble Christ, just as Eve's sons resemble their fallen progenitor. In this way, once again, the divine image is restored by a rebirth: the Christian's fundamental resemblance to Jesus is achieved at baptism, and is continued by obedience to the Church's teachings.

In one image-sequence, therefore, the work of Christ's Atonement is portrayed as the restoration of a divine image: herein, in a sense, the entire economy of salvation is embodied, at least as it affects the individual. But for many Fathers the culmination of this process is only achieved in the mystical ascent of the soul to God. And it is this imagery, so intimately bound up with the former, that we now propose to discuss.

The mystical doctrine of the early Church was deeply influenced by the symbols of Platonic philosophy and its attempt to free the soul of matter by the contemplation of the pure ideas. But the Platonism which was to some degree absorbed by the Fathers of the Church had already passed through that peculiar prism called Neo-Platonism, known to us chiefly from the works of Plotinus in the edition of Porphyry,[21] the few dry treatises left by Porphyry himself, Proclus, and the mysterious Dionysius the Areopagite.

It was the year 232, about the time that Origen left Alexandria to take up residence in Palestine, that an Egyptian Greek named Plotinus, from the city of Lycopolis in Upper Egypt, began to attend the lectures of the Platonist Ammonius Saccas at Alexandria. It was an occasion filled with great consequences for the history of Christian philosophy. For though a number of Christians had sat at the feet of Ammonius, no one was to have the influence which Plotinus was to achieve after his death. Sometime after Saccas' death, Plotinus went on the expedition under the emperor Gordian against the Persians. Returning from the campaign, he settled at Rome and straightway gathered around him a coterie of Greeks, Romans, and Orientals, among whom were the emperor Gallienus, his wife Salonina, and the ascetic thinker who was to be Plotinus' Boswell, the Tyrian Porphyry. Gallienus and his wife had even planned to found a small utopian colony in

[21] See *Plotinus: The Enneads,* transl. by Stephen MacKenna, revised by B. S. Page, with foreword by E. R. Dodds and Introduction by Paul Henry (London, 1956), especially the Introduction, pp. xxxiii *ff*. *Cf*. also the discussion of Plotinus by Karl Jaspers, *Die grossen Philosophen* (Munich, 1957), vol. I, 656 *ff*.

Italy based on the doctrines of Neo-Platonism, but by Plotinus' death in 270, nothing had gone forward. Indeed, Plotinus' own lectures, or rather, informal discussions, remained in a disordered state until Porphyry, at his master's behest, began to collect, edit, and publish them. The resultant work, grouped artificially into six books of nine treatises each, was called the *Enneads,* or literally, "the sets of nine." For the Neo-Platonists, this book became a second Bible; for the ultimate goal of the system was immediate communion with the Divine, a state that Plotinus, on Porphyry's word, had attained only four times during the six years of his discipleship.

In the Neo-Platonists, the worst tendencies of the early school are somewhat counterbalanced by an authentic emphasis on a religious, even mystical, approach to the problem of God and the transcendent. But if there is a more deeply religious element in Neo-Platonism, as opposed to the philosophic piety of Socrates, the Neo-Platonists seem even more deeply shocked at the infinite complexity and mystery of matter—the world of the concrete and of experience—and they employ various methods in order to effect the Platonic flight from reality into the dream-world of introspection. "The soul has become ugly," says Plotinus, "by being immersed in what is not itself, by its descent into the body." This is the cardinal doctrine of Plotinian meditation. Here in the Never-Never Land of introspection, the artificial withdrawal from the world's immediate and urgent stimuli tends to create the delusion of calm, impassive truth, complete control over the body's drives and needs. One gets the impression that the Plotinian meditation was a concentration on certain images which produced a state of self-hypnosis.

In any case, the core of their teaching was the so-called Ladder of Being, which graphically demonstrated how the gap could be bridged between the pure spirit of the Divine and Matter which was the source of all evil and metaphysical corruption. The underlying imagery seems now to be a ladder or staircase (as it is in Plato's *Symposium,* in the picture given by the lady Diotima); now the concentric ripples on the surface of water which proceed outward from the center with a gradually diminishing power. As the Reality of the universe proceeds downward (by stages) or outward (as ripples), there are three grades of Being: Mind or *Nous,* the World-Soul, and finally Nature. It is Mind which, in a single timeless self-intuition, possesses all the Platonic ideas of things. The World-Soul, because of its weaker unity, must apprehend all things discursively; and it is this successive thinking of the Soul which results in the formation of Time and Space. The last principle in the divine hierarchy—making four—is *Physis* or Nature. Her thinking is a kind of dreaming, a succession of images: and the result of this dream is the physical, sensual world. Man is for Plotinus a microcosm, combining in himself all the elements of the divine hypostases: the One, mind, soul, nature, and matter. How the human soul descended and became imprisoned in matter, this Plotinus never really explains. But man, by a reversion to his Source, by a kind of mystical ecstasy, is meant to become aware of his divinity, and eventually by meditation and by virtuous acts become like unto the perfection of the Godhead. For Plotinus, there is no clear concept of moral guilt or evil, no explanation of the conflict between man's drives and his ideals, no clear notion of freedom, deliberate malice or the need of asceticism. It is, in general, an optimistic mysticism.

Plotinianism especially influenced those Fathers who were dissatisfied with the externalism of Alexandrian asceticism, and longed for a more philosophic substratum for the truths of Christian revelation. It was Plotinus' doctrine of Reversion to the Divine which had the most important influence upon the patristic writers. For Plotinus, however, it should be recalled that the entire process is a kind of natural redemption without Christ; an almost Buddhist act of self-awareness and the comprehension of Zen. The Plotinian One is perfect, remote, aloof, and has no relationship with mortality; it is the soul's central need to make the Divine its center, indeed to realize the presence of the Divine within it. By a peculiar mental effort the soul, by stripping away all obstacles, can achieve this act of inward unity. When it does, it is momentarily at least identified with the supreme Unity of the One. "This is the good," says Plotinus in the sixth *Ennead,* "and there is no better."

Now it was precisely the Plotinian concept of Reversion which attracted the Fathers of the Church. Sometimes, as in Methodius of Olympus' *Symposium*—a transposition of Plato's dialogue to the realm of supernatural love and chastity—the Return of the soul is clothed in the imagery of the soul's chariot taken from Plato's *Phaedrus.* In Plato it was the Ride of the Gods which men try to follow in chariots drawn by two horses, Spirit and Desire; but only a relatively few men can control their animals long enough to reach the rim of the world and there contemplate the Ideas. Most, after rising a bit, fall back down again. In Methodius this upward flight from matter is achieved by the practice of chastity. By a supreme effort the charioteer of the soul directs the chariot upward to the vault of heaven, and there "they stand and gaze directly upon Immortality itself as it wells up from the pure bosom of the Almighty." For the ascetical writers, the release of the spirit can only be accomplished by bodily austerity and privation; it is this, says John Chrysostom, that "makes the soul clear and brighter; it gives it wings, and makes it light and ready to soar aloft." It is only by an austere regime, he tells us, that we can "make the soul more transparent, her wings light, her bonds looser." But with the more mystical writers—Methodius, Gregory of Nyssa and Dionysius the Areopagite—the process is less violent, less ascetical, and less austere.

Methodius lays great stress on the intellectual apprehension of the meaning of the Church's teaching, and throughout his *Symposium* he proposes for consideration a number of imaginative visions for the young women and widows who were under his care. Despite the Asiatic intensity of Methodius' work, it is doubtful that it was mystical in the strict sense. For this one would require some evidence of transport, ecstasy; perhaps even a vision of the Godhead somehow transcending the grasp of the imagination and the mind. But Methodius' visions, for all their poetic beauty, are imaginative; indeed, he urges his maidens to use their imaginations in order to think of heaven "even from afar." With this primacy of the imagination in Methodius, it seems almost certain that any mystical experience should be excluded. In fact, in all the writings of those who pretend to give mystical instruction, there is always the danger that their description of ecstasy is largely drawn from their imaginations.

Even Origen's symbols for the mystical life might well be purely imaginative. He speaks of the rise of the soul to Mt. Thabor, then the embrace of the Word and the spiritual kiss with which He receives the soul. It is a mystical marriage between the soul and the Crucified, consummated amid blinding light, the glory of His radiance. Origen was among the first of the Fathers to apply the Song of Songs, with its sensuous love imagery, to the union of the soul with Christ. Indeed, the explicitness of his applications seems to us today almost embarrassing. But there is no certain ground for accepting any of this as more than a kind of literary or imaginative mysticism: a Christian adaptation of the Plotinian union.

Methodius' allegories are even more visual, though less explicitly sensual. For him it is not so much the individual soul as the Church that is the Spouse of Christ, the virgin Mother of the faithful; and the souls of the chaste are meant to participate in a marriage procession on the last day which leads up to the Gates of Life. The apparel of the bride is taken to be the interior virtues; and the secrets of Christianity are revealed when the Bride and Groom conduct the souls of the just into the heavenly marriage chamber. The Church conceives the just during the mystical sleep of the Cross. The baptized are nourished on doctrine at the bosom of their Mother until they are brought to perfection. In urging his consecrated virgins to raise their thoughts to heaven, Methodius tells them of the heavenly meadows, bright with every kind of flower, shrub and tree. The trees are, in fact, the archetypal virtues, which men on earth possess imperfectly—a doctrine that we find also in Porphyry. The Eden that is heaven is lit by mystical lights that form patterns, washed by fresh streams and fragrant with perfume. And there men, as they gaze on the Godhead, will join in an antiphonal chant with the angelic choirs.

On earth, however, the soul must pilot a ship in a stormy sea; and the waves of the senses create confusion and doubt. It must struggle, wrestle, with the powers of evil that attempt to ensnare the just and take them captive. The ecstatic Rise of the soul to the rim of the world must ultimately be supported by a life of fortitude—which is, for Methodius, the essence of all human virtue—and, ideally, by a chaste life, a daily martyrdom. At the end, with the resurrection of the body, Christ will come to reign over all men in a Millenium of Rest, at the end of which He will lead his Church on the clouds of the East, to the heavenly Paradise.

Towards the close of the *Symposium* there is a beautiful hymn in rhythmic iambic which is the marriage-song of the virgins as they accompany Christ and his spouse, the Church, to the heavenly bridal chamber. It begins with a refrain:

> Chastely I live for Thee,
> And holding my lighted lamps,
> My Spouse, I go forth to meet Thee.

The scene is on the Last Day; the trumpet heralds the coming of the King:

> From heaven has come the sound that wakes the dead,
> Bidding us go to meet our Spouse in the east
> With all speed, in white, our lamps alight. Awake,
> Before the King enters the gates!

Thecla, the leader of the choir, then goes on to narrate the difficulties she experienced in living the life of virginity: her renouncement of marriage, family, and wealth. Thus,

> I have escaped the Dragon's countless wiles,
> O Blessed One! Awaiting Thy final coming,
> I have braved fire and flame and ravenous beasts.

To Mother Church, the Spouse, she sings:

> O Queen arrayed in beauty, receive us too
> With open door within thy bridal bower.
> Bride of unsullied body, triumphing, lovely!
> At His side we stand in robes like thine, to sing,
> O Virgin, of thy blessed nuptials.

The wedding banquet stands ready; bowls of immortal nectar are on the table. But before entering in, Thecla sings of all the heroes and heroines of Scripture who showed their courage in the struggle against the flesh. Now as they enter Paradise,

> Death is made captive, all folly crushed;
> Dead all heart-melting grief. And all at once
> The lamp of God's good pleasure has shone on men.

At last Mother Church, the Queen, enters in, and the virgin choir accompanies her, bearing white lilies, bathed in light. The song ends:

> Behold we are come! Receive us too, O Father
> With Thy Servant within the Gates of Life.

The dramatic intensity of Thecla's hymn foreshadows the more complex acrostics of Romanos, the Melodos of Constantinople. It is, indeed, a hymn of great majesty and stands as an achievement of the primitive Asiatic Church.

Thecla's hymn does, indeed, summarize all the symbolism and allegory of Methodius' *Symposium.* All his imagery forms an ellipse revolving about two focal points: the love, comfort, and peace of There; and the austerity and struggle of Here. Thus he associates with heaven all the comforting, sensual images drawn from life and nature: luxuriant gardens, love, marriage, and procreation; with earth, on the other hand, all the images of discomfort: pain, sorrow, battle, struggle, the sea. The entire *Symposium,* and not merely the closing hymn, is a kind of exotic prose poetry. But there is no evidence that it reflects mystical experience in the strict sense of the word.

Gregory of Nyssa, on the other hand, offers us the first real evidence of mysticism, especially in his didactic *Life of Moses* and in the series of lyrical homilies gathered together as a *Commentary on the Song of Songs.* In Gregory the ideal of perfection becomes the flight of the soul towards the archetypal Beauty that is God. The flight, the rise of the chariot-soul, the climbing of Mount Sinai amid thunder and smoke—this is Gregory's adaptation of the Plotinian ecstasy along the lines of the Alexandrian tradition. In the *Life of Moses* there are three stages of Moses' approach to the Godhead: first in the light, then in the cloud, and finally in the darkness of Sinai. In the final stage of mystical vision, Moses does not see the face of God, but rather learns the truth about His nature amid fire and smoke, in the cloud which Dionysius the Areopagite later called the Darkness of Unknowing (*Mystical Theology* 1.3). For Moses, seeing God is not seeing Him; loving Him is the never attaining or touching Him in the Darkness, but ever going on and on as His devoted servant. As Gregory tells us:

> What is the meaning of Moses' entrance into the darkness? . . . The Word here teaches us that . . . the more the soul progresses in contemplation, the more it becomes aware that the divine nature is invisible. . . . Here is the true knowledge of that which the soul is seeking, and this is its vision: in seeing that it cannot see, because that which it seeks transcends all vision, enveloped as it were on all sides by a dark impenetrability.

This is the night that the soul experiences according to Gregory's *Commentary on the Song of Songs:* "By night on my bed I sought him whom my soul loveth . . . but I found him not" (*Cant.* 3.1). As Gregory explains this passage:

> Leaving all created things, and abandoning all help from the intellect, I have found my Beloved by faith alone.

This intuition of the Godhead, says Gregory, causes the soul to go out of itself in a state of joyful ecstasy at the presence of the divinity, however invisible and perceived only by faith. At times Gregory calls the experience a kind of intoxication, a sober drunkenness, following an expression found in Philo of Alexandria. In this transport by which God is somehow present to the soul in the Darkness the senses reel, and yet we are not drunk; or again, we are as though in a sound sleep, and yet fully awake. Indeed, the whole experience cannot be explained or communicated because of our human weakness. Again Gregory tries to explain it as a kind of waking sleep, in which the soul seems to lose consciousness of all else save the manifestation of the Godhead.

In the *Commentary on the Song of Songs* he also develops the climbing symbol: in our approach to God we feel we are on a never-ending ladder, or on a cliff of infinite height with a view of indefinite numbers of hills still to be climbed beyond. Thus the senses become confused; and we experience a spiritual vertigo, a dizziness, as we come closer and ever closer to the Divinity, as though we were on the edge of a cliff, looking down into an endless abyss. And all the while the intimate presence of God, together with His ultimate unattainability, arouses a sharp pang of love in the soul: it is a thirst that becomes always more intense by drinking, or, again, a kind of arrow-wound that grows only more painful as we try to heal it. Once the soul catches a glimpse of the Beloved in the Darkness, it despairs of ever completely attaining what it desires; for though "mortally wounded by love," it sees that the divine Beauty is ultimately inaccessible. Frustration and delicious ecstasy form the polarity of the privileged soul's espousals with God.

The problems connected with Gregory's presentation of mystical experience need not concern us here. His handling of the Greek text of the *Song of Songs,* so traditional within the Alexandrian sphere of influence, at times creates confusion if not contradiction. Again, the relationship between the theological and merely psychological aspects of the mystical phenomena is not always clear. At times the soul's intoxication and dizziness seem to come, not from a special intuition of the Godhead, but rather from the philosophical awareness that God cannot be comprehended, that He is infinitely transcendent. Indeed, the indefinite progression of the soul in quest of God, the never resting, the constant recession and withdrawal of the Godhead—all this suggests an obscurantism which is hard to reconcile with modern theological doctrine. And yet, despite his flaws, Gregory offers the most penetrating attempt in the entire early patristic period to grasp and describe the mystical experience, and the phrases adapted from the *Song of Songs* become current coin down to the Spanish, Flemish, and German mystics of the high Renascence. This transformation of the sensuous love-songs of the Canticle into a highly structured theological framework is sometimes perplexing to the modern scholar, and is further proof of the distance that separates us from the imaginative atmosphere of the patristic period.

It must however be emphasized that though Gregory and Dionysius follow Origen's theory of allegorism and the higher, spiritual senses of the soul, they both withdraw more and more from the sensuous imagery of the Canticle. In a most instructive passage in the introduction to his *Commentary,* Gregory carefully explains to the lady Olympias that the vivid language of the Song, the embraces, kisses and touches, are always to be taken as experiences in the spiritual order, as phenomena of the spiritual senses of the soul. This is clear from the first homily on the Song of Songs:

> The words of the Spirit teach us that we have spiritual functions and operations on an analogy with our bodily senses. We can distinguish wine and milk by taste. But there is also a spiritual power of the soul which apprehends their meaning on a spiritual level. So too a kiss is a function of the sense of touch: in kissing, two pairs of lips meet. But so too there is a spiritual sense of touch whch operates on the divine message, and is actuated by a spiritual, incorporeal contact. . . . Similarly there is a sense which inhales the fragrance of the divine perfume; this does not use the nostrils, but is a kind of immaterial, spiritual faculty which, by an inhalation of the soul, draws in the sweet odor of Christ.

In this way, therefore, the application suggested by the sacred text are made, and the hidden meanings are perceived by the spiritual senses; but it is also by these senses that the soul is more closely united to God and to the spiritual realities of the Christian dispensation. It is thus that sensuous reality, in Gregory, finds its place within the mystical life: as a symbol, shadow, and cipher. Thus Gregory foreshadows the spirituality of the later Byzantine writers and, to a degree, the mysticism of certain modern Russian and Oriental teachers.

Of the later writers, it is Dionysius the Areopagite that comes closest to Gregory in style and conception. While pseudo-Dionysius is at once more ecstatic and transported, his imagery is even less sensuous than Gregory's. In psuedo-Dionysius the mystical process is perhaps even clearer than it is in Gregory; for he is less encumbered with the homiletic requirements of the Scriptural commentary. But in pseudo-Dionysius we have again the basic Plotinian Rise of the soul to the darkness of the One, though here it is achieved within the Christian context: it is God, not the soul, Who must take the first step. And as the soul turns in upon itself, it more and more throws off the impurities of matter; and as it becomes aware of its true self it rises to an intuition of the Godhead, the Superessence, under a Cloud of Unknowing.

As in Gregory, the mystical experience is always Christian, its background always the Biblical revelation of the divinity.

In the mystical theology of Gregory and pseudo-Dionysius we see the culmination of the image-doctrine of the early Fathers. For the divine image of God in man is only fully restored when, after being incorporated into Christ, man becomes aware of his true self and his kinship with God at the height of mystical union. Even within the social framework of the Church God approaches each man as an individual image of Himself and communicates Himself wordlessly in Darkness.

We have, up till now, confined ourselves almost exclusively to the Eastern tradition. And indeed it was the theology of Origen, Gregory, and Dionysius which ultimately established the pattern for all mystical symbolism in the West throughout the Middle Ages and the Renascence. As always, the western tradition was almost wholly derivative, with the exception of Augustine, who drew his inspiraton more directly from a reading of Plotinus and the Neo-Platonists. The Franciscan devotional revival made its own contribution, but this we shall leave to a later chapter.

The Western Tradition

The Latin patristic writers did not, in general, broaden the mystical horizons inherited from the Greek tradition. Here as in other areas Greek insight spoke first and Latin practice followed after. Ambrose, in the treatises he wrote for his sister Marcellina and her group of consecrated virgins at Milan,[22] borrows from the nuptial imagery of Hippolytus and the other Greek writers with great freedom. Basic to all were the elusive and fragmentary love-poems of the *Song of Songs:* the call to love, the symbols of spring, the garden of delights with its flowers and heady perfumes, the clothing of the maiden and her beloved, the anxious dreams, the knock at the gate, the spiritual embrace. For Ambrose, of course, the ideal of the Christian, the perfect restora-

[22] See F. Holmes Dudden, *The Life and Times of St. Ambrose* (2 vols., Oxford, 1935), I.133 *ff.*; on the origin and dates of the treatises, II.695 *ff.*

tion of the divine image, lay only in the life of virginity. The symbol of the perfectly chaste life for Ambrose is the bee (*On Virgins I*, 40–43), that lives a life constantly on the wing, ever busy in the garden of Jesus, sucking the honey of the divine word. It is a passage of great beauty, reminiscent of Vergil's eulogy of the bee in the fourth Georgic:

> The virgin is rightly compared to the bee, for she should, like her, be ever busy, ever chaste. The bee knows not sex; feeding on the dew, it makes its honey. So the virgin's dew is God's word, which comes down to earth like the dew. The virgin's chastity is her inviolate body, and what she brings forth is the fruit of her lips, a speech full of sweetness and ignorant of bitterness. . . . My daughter, imitate the bee. . . . And I will show you the flower to pluck: it is He Who said: I am a flower of the field, and a lily of the valleys, as a lily among thorns.

Or again, departing from the mystical imagery of the Canticle, Ambrose compares the virgin to the altar of incense (*On Virgins* II.18) in the Temple of Moses, to the Christian altars

> on which Christ is daily immolated for the redemption of the body. Indeed, if the virgin's body is a temple, her soul is surely an altar on which, covered by the hands of the eternal Priest, her own burning members breathe forth the perfume of a divine fire.

In the vivid style of the treatises on virginity we catch a glimpse of the genius that created the Ambrosian hymns. And yet, Ambrose's treatises, for all their beauty, are patchwork collections of sermons stocked with the imagery he had largely borrowed from earlier writers. He is, above all, eminently practical: he encourages no illusions in the young ladies under his care. They are exhorted to all the maidenly virtues; their doors should be kept locked to all but Christ, and they must devote themselves to the Scriptures, liturgical piety, prayer, and fasting. Their lives must be offered in reparation for their parents' sins, and for the sins of the world (*Exhortation to Virginity* 11.76):

> There must be no unrestrained joy among our virgins.

> And if they have nothing to weep for, they should weep for the world, for the sins of the wicked.

And finally, Ambrose, practical Roman to the end, bids his charges not to be misled by the imagery of the *Song of Songs;* he urges them to be aware of the psychological need of such an introduction to a life of stern obligation and austerity. The horse must be gently patted before we apply the yoke and the spur; the good woman must be gently courted before marriage (*On Virgins* II, 41);

> So too our virgin may amuse herself at first with pious love, and marvel at the golden supports of the heavenly couch at the threshold of her nuptials, and examine the posts decorated with garlands of green sprigs, and enjoy to the full the delightful songs of the choir—and all this that she may not shy away in terror at the Lord's yoke, before she has even answered His call. Hence the words, Come from Lebanon, my bride; come from Lebanon.

The mystic bridal bed of Solomon, he tells them, is nothing less than an introduction, an allure, to entice them into the disciplined ways of the chaste Christian life.

Perhaps the most important Latin commentary on the Canticle came from the pen of St. Bernard of Clairvaux (1090–1153).[23] Born near Dijon of knightly parents, Bernard entered the newly-formed community at Citeaux. His very presence attracted, it is said, so many vocations that it was decided that he found a new monastery at Clairvaux in 1115. It was as Abbot of Clairvaux that Bernard was to wield an incomparable influence upon the

[23] On Bernard, see Max Manitius, *Geschichte der lateinischen Literatur des Mittelalters* (Munich, 1931), III.123 *ff*.; and F. J. E. Raby, *A History of Christian-Latin Poetry from the Beginnings to the Close of the Middle Ages* (Oxford, 1927), pp. 326 *ff*., with the literature cited. On the foundation of Clairvaux, see W. W. Williams, *Studies in St. Bernard of Clairvaux* (London, 1927), pp. 107 *ff*. On the entire period, see Etienne Gilson, *History of Christian Philosophy in the Middle Ages* (New York, 1955), especially, on St. Bernard, pp. 164–171, with the valuable notes and bibliography to date, pp. 630–32; *cf*. also the more popular but extremely useful summary by Gordon Leff, *Medieval Thought from Saint Augustine to Okham* (Penguin Books, 1958), esp. pp. 133 *ff*.

Church of the twelfth century. Driven, as it were, by an inner fire, Bernard attacked both the philosophic rationalism and the growing sensuality of European Christendom. But at heart he shared the devotional simplicity of Francis of Assisi: the ultimate object of his mystical prayer was the humanity of Jesus and the sacred Side that poured forth blood and water. His series of eighty-four *Sermons on the Song of Songs,* delivered for the most part in the year 1135, though often diffuse, blend this Cistercian devotion to Christ with the traditional Alexandrian-Plotinian interpretation of the Canticle.

These remarkable sermons, which incorporate the bulk of his mystical theology, were delivered most probably in the chapter room at Citeaux; and the choir monks who first heard them were an unusually privileged audience. Bernard draws from many traditional sources, not least among them being Ambrose and Augustine. But though Bernard is at times more sensuous and more moralistic and practical than his predecessors, his exegesis is inferior, often lacking sharpness and focus. The allegorism of the *Sermons* comprises four levels. For Bernard the beloved Shulamite of the Canticle is now the virgin Church, now the monastic congregation before him, now the sinner struggling to keep the commandments, and finally the privileged soul of the mystic caught up in the ecstatic embrace of Christ. The audience is thus a wide one: for some of the sermons must surely have been intended for the people and the clergy at large, especially those which deal with contemporary scandals and doctrinal heresies.

Bernard loosely follows the Vulgate text of the Canticle,[24]

[24] Though scholars still dispute on the origins of the collection known as the *Song of Songs* (i.e., "the most precious of songs"), most today would tend to hold that it is not a drama—as Gregory of Nyssa and the Alexandrian school at times seem to take it. It is indeed a collection of dramatic poems or songs attributed to different voices, with fragmentary snatches of others; but modern editors group them in many different ways. The best account of the history of the exegesis will be found in H. H. Rowley, *The Servant of the Lord and Other Essays on the Old Testament* (London, 1954), pp. 187–234; see also the discussion and bibliographies in Robert H. Pfeiffer, *Introduction to the Old Testament* (London, 1952), pp. 708 *ff.*; his later, summary volume, *The Books of the Old Testament* (New York,

pausing to make his applications as he goes. It is beautiful to watch him rise from the foundations of an Augustinian asceticism and ecclesiology to the height of mystical contemplation. Christ is the royal Spouse and Shepherd who feeds his beloved bride, embraces her by grace and kisses her with the kiss of peace. Of the three kisses which the Lord allows the Christian—the kiss on the feet, the kiss on the hands, and the kiss on the mouth—only the last is permitted to those who are in the unitive way. Bernard constantly distinguishes between the spiritual and the sensuous love of the Savior; but to the modern reader perhaps the difference may not always be clear, and one tends to blend into the other. But we must always recall that, under the sensuous imagery, Bernard is always speaking of the invisible operation of grace. Even in that lovely passage in the ninth Sermon, where he speaks of the embrace of Jesus and his bride, the Church:

> He gives her the kiss she has longed for. . . . And so great is the power of that kiss that she at once conceives and her bosom swells with milk. . . . So too we approach the altar of God and pray and, if we but persevere, despite our own dryness and tepidity, grace will overpower us, our bosom will swell, love will fill our hearts . . . and the milk of sweetness will overflow everywhere in a torrent.

And so the luxuriant, almost Oriental imagery continues in a remarkable fertility. The King's great bed is the Virgin's holy womb; but his final resting place is the tomb from which He rose to embrace his bride the Church. For this is the bride who is black but beautiful, who feeds her flock from the bosom of her charity and grace. The loveliness of the spouse comes from her supernatural goodness: her eyes flash with the moral virtues, and the spikenard that exhales from her garments are devotion, piety, sorrow for sin. We too, like the bride of the Canticle, must tend

---

1957), pp. 217 *ff.*; and H. Lusseau's balanced account in *Introduction à la Bible,* I.655–66. Pfeiffer distinguishes nine groups of songs or love-idylls; Lusseau divides the book into a *prologue* (1.2–4); *five poems,* divided as follows: 1.5–2.7, 2.8–3.5, 2.6–5.1; 5.2–6.3; 6.4–9.4; a *dénouement* (8.5–7), and two *appendices* (8.8–14).

our flocks at noon, and keep watch over the gate of the senses. Jesus' presence is as a constant fragrance: the bundle of myrrh that hangs as a sachet on her breast is the lingering thought of Christ Crucified. Linger, says Bernard to his flock, on the exotic landscape of the Song, with its fragrant trees and rare flowers, on the hills blossoming with the springtime: for here is the Church, with its doctrines, its sacraments, and its liturgy. For it is here that we shall hear the voice of the Beloved, leaping upon the mountains, skipping upon the hills—the eternal Shepherd in constant quest for the souls of men. For the privileged soul who rises at his call, his embrace brings ecstasy, his kiss a sleep of mystic transport.

Bernard's *Sermons* are an important key to unlock the mysteries of the Middle Ages. For all their emotion, they reflect a magnificent, quiet grandeur, and in them the Hebraic imagery lives once again, much as the stories of the Old Testament shine with a new light in the stained-glass windows of Chartres alongside of the pictures of Christ and Our Lady. It is in this way that the symbols of the *Song of Songs* revitalize the growing Christian sentiment of mediaeval monasticism.

But it is not our purpose to enter into the mystical ideas of Gregory, Dionysius, and Bernard, nor their doctrine of the spiritual senses and the mystical heightening of awareness in the superior reason. Suffice it to say that all, or most, of the imagery was by now established which would serve the later mediaeval and Renascence mystics as a vehicle for their recorded transports. One must, of course, always beware of confusion in the subtle combination of Plotinian ideas and Jewish-Christian symbolism. For the Christian does not always look upon a retreat from the world as the most fruitful mode of knowledge; nor is matter for us, as it was for Plotinus and Dionysius, the source of evil and corruption. For the Christian matter is rather the presentation of the infinite richness and fecundity of the universe; and the only true evil is the bad will of man.

In a certain sense, the symbols which the mystical writers offer us can be read on two levels: on the one, it is the story of a soul in mystic transport, endowed with the special operation of the gifts of the Holy Spirit. This is the level we find in Gregory,

Dionysius, and perhaps in Origen. But there is a second level which becomes clear in Ambrose and Bernard—the Latin Church was always more practical—wherein the ascent of Sinai and the embrace of the Spouse merely symbolize the ordinary life of the faithful soul. And the images of rise, love, ecstasy, and embrace express the constant struggle to approach the Transcendent by the good Christian life. As Ambrose had said, the image of the divine nuptials are perhaps useful at the outset—"lest the soul retreat in terror before she has begun"—but, once initial barriers are overcome, the soul has less need for symbols.

As we follow the growth of patristic ascetical and mystical doctrine, it becomes clear that the Christian's ultimate struggle is pitched within the depths of his own soul, in the choosing from moment to moment the best of the drives and inclinations which rise up in our consciousness. The constant battle that this entails, and the constant need of a supernatural assistance—this is, after all, what the Fathers have constantly spoken of under various images. Ambrose again reminds us: "We cannot imitate God" (*Deum imitari non possumus*). But we know the quarter where the Transcendent lies, what direction the struggle will take, what ultimate victory would be like. The distance to the horizon, Gregory of Nyssa tells us, seems infinite. Yet we can only be what He intends us to be. Whether the soul's ultimate path will be, as it was for Bernard, beyond the normal avenues of sacramental grace, into realms that require mystical gifts, only He can decide.

The Catechesis of St. Augustine

CHAPTER SIX

AS A former teacher of literature and rhetoric, it was natural for Augustine to rethink traditional doctrine and to project it once more on a personal imaginative level. What has remained perhaps unnoticed hitherto is precisely this great imaginative sweep in his presentation of the mysteries of Christianity. "Since men are often stubborn in being convinced of the truth, and since it is the rare soul that sees the objective truth in itself," he tells us in his work *De ordine*, "we must not only instruct men but also move their emotions deeply." So, too, in the treatise *On Christian Doctrine*, though he stresses the primacy of intellectual conviction, he leaves wide room for the emotional appeal. Augustine himself was a man of deep feelings; and it is clear from his works that his endeavor was not to manipulate the emotions of men, but rather to present Christianity as he saw it, and as he had emotionally experienced it. As grace was for him an overpowering delight, so too the deep wisdom which was the ultimate insight of Christianity was never purely a cold intellectual process, but the response of the whole man. Thus in Augustine, *Sapientia*, Wisdom, which is the culmination of the Christian life, is not a mere Platonic vision of the Ideas; it is a loving awareness of the place of Christ and the Church in the pattern of salvation. It is the keystone of the entire intellectual structure that he so laboriously erected.[25]

[25] For a good introduction to the life and thought of St. Augustine, see Vernon J. Bourke, *Augustine's Quest of Wisdom: Life and Phi-*

His unique imaginative genius is especially revealed in the *Confessions* and in the *City of God*. But the structure of both of these difficult works is apt to be misunderstood, so original are they in their departure from the normal catechetical techniques which Augustine himself expounded in *On Catechizing the Uninstructed*. The *Confessions* were apparently written at the request of members of the Latin hierarchy (some have suggested Paulinus, Bishop of Nola) who desired to have an account of Augustine's life for the edification of their congregations. The ultimate clue has not yet been revealed, save that we know that Augustine was working on the book around the years 398–400; years which coincide with his works on *Genesis* and on several books against the Manichaeans. He speaks of them as the "thirteen books of *My Confessions*," in the *Retractations* (2.6), that "praise the just and good God for whatever is good and evil in me, and attempt to raise man's mind and heart to Him" (*in eum excitant humanum intellectum et affectum*). What is important about this description is that, first of all, the entire work is considered an integral unit, and not merely the biographical 2–9; secondly, Augustine stresses that the main purpose of the book is *laus* and *excitatio*, to praise God (for the work of salvation in the sinner Augustine) and to excite men to know and love Him.

Here the meaning of the word *confessio* becomes clear, even if it were not verified from the opening words of the prologue: *Magnus es, domine, et laudabilis valde*, "Thou art great, O Lord, and most worthy of praise." Augustine himself explains the meaning of the word, in his *Commentary on the Psalms:* "Confession is not only for sin but also for praise." The book of *My Confessions* is then a series of acts of praise, which celebrate the wonderful acts of God—almost like liturgical preface—culminating in the

---

losophy of the Bishop of Hippo (Milwaukee, 1947). For a discussion of some of Augustine's important ideas, one should consult Ladner, *The Idea of Reform*, pp. 153 *ff*. and *passim*, with the bibliography; in Ladner's view, the mediaeval concept of theological and moral reform was basically Augustinian, although he admits that conflicting streams of thought continued to prevail. On Augustine, see also Gilson, *History of Christian Philosophy*, pp. 70–81, with the relevant notes; and G. Leff, *Medieval Thought*, pp. 32–54.

raising up of the sinner, Augustine. The *laudes Domini,* however, are directed to God in such wise that men might overhear for their own edification: "To whom do I tell this story? I tell it before Thee for the sake of my people and for the whole human race" (*Conf.* 2.3). And the reason: "that all may realize the depths from which man cries to Thee." It is, then, an epic of the human soul; a concrete symbol of the message of Salvation. Thus the hagiographical element is secondary—even perhaps distorted.

It was also perhaps Augustine's intention to deprecate himself and to offset to some degree the great popularity and influence which his personality and his writings exercised even in his lifetime. Thus, in an account which emphasizes more strongly the biographical element of the *Confessions,* he writes to Darius, a minister of Valentinian III (*Epist.* 231): "Please accept a copy of *My Confessions,* as you asked for them. There you will see me, so that you will not praise me beyond what I am; believe what I say of myself, and not what others say of me." Thus, in both of Augustine's descriptions of his work, in the *Retractations* and in the letter to Count Darius, we see the two aspects of the *Confessions* placed in their proper perspective, the biographical and the catechetical. Though the majority of scholars seem convinced that Augustine's past life was exaggerated, and that the work does not give a fair picture of his attitude of mind at the very time he was composing the treatise *On the Happy Life,* we can perhaps never be sure of the exact degree of distortion and improper emphasis.

But the problem is best solved by considering the *Confessions* as a quite original variant of the primitive catechetical technique, which had, as we have said in an earlier chapter, two main sections: the *narration,* or historical account of God's favors towards men since the beginning of the world; and the *exhortation,* in which the catechumens would be urged to apply the story to themselves and to put on, as Augustine said, the "habits of Jesus," by becoming a fervent Christian. Augustine's originality consisted in varying this technique as follows: the entire discourse (narration and exhortation) is now delivered as a *confessio* (or, in the Greek, *exhomologêsis*), or a series of confessions or "elevations," in which God is publicly praised for what He did in the life of the sinner Augustine; secondly, Augustine himself becomes the typical sinner, raised up "from the depths" by the power of God. He is the convert confessing his experience; but he wishes to broaden and expand it into an instructive tract on the supernatural operation of God in the soul.

The whole work becomes much easier to understand when seen in this light. After the prologue, 1.1–6, which sets the tone of the *confessio laudis*, the "confession of praise," we have the narrative of the conversion up to book 9; book 10 is another prayerful confession from Augustine the sinner, as he reflects upon his entire life; then books 11–13 further continue the meditation on God and Time, on God as the soul's ultimate Quest. The context of the last three books shifts to Augustine's exegetical meditations on the book of *Genesis:* for it is in the creation-story, the Hexaemeron, that Augustine now sees the ultimate meaning of the world and of Christianity. Though not in strict logic connected with the confession-theme as he had conceived it at the outset–Augustine always felt free to shift emphases and contexts throughout the course of a work–the last chapters are still "confessions" ultimately intended for the instruction of the faithful. The polarity, God-Sinner, now comes to its ultimate term in the Rest which the Lord took on the seventh day after His work of creation was completed. It is God, the Alpha and Omega, the beginning and the end of Time; and once again the minor theme, Augustine's conversion, fades into the background before the inscrutable and immutable majesty of the triune Diety.

A similar catechetical technique is observable in the *City of God.* The sprawling nature of the work is due, in no small measure, to the fact that it appeared in at least six installments from A.D. 413 to 426. Again, the polemic nature of Part 1 (books 1–10) makes it difficult to recognize the structure which better emerges in Part 2 (11–22), the more catechetical section. Augustine begins with the symbolism we have already seen in the *Apocalypse:* the heavenly Jerusalem and the wickedness of Babylon (Rome). But for him the notion of cities is enlarged into that of *civitas,* or citizenship, in the legal Roman sense. For a man could enjoy Roman citizenship, or franchise, no matter what his race or nationality, no matter what part of the Roman world he lived in.

So Augustine's two citizenships comprise (as he tells us in the *City of God* 15.2) "two sorts of men, those who live by men's values (*secundum hominem*), and those who live according to God's values (*secundum Deum*), and these two we call, mystically, Cities." States, or empires, or citizenships, would perhaps be a better translation. Even so, the meaning of each City constantly shifts: the City of Earth is now the wicked of the world, now the Roman empire, now the damned; the City of God is sometimes the Church, sometimes all the good, sometimes those who are predestined for heaven. The extension of each term rests on a constantly sliding scale.

But what Augustine has done is to combine two parallel histories: for each City he treats the origin, the progress on earth, and the Last End. It is, once again, the catechetical narrative, only now on two levels; and the virtues and vices are more graphically presented. Though its primary purpose is not philosophical, the *City of God* does present on a broad canvas the first Christian philosophy—or, rather, theology—of history. It is the Christian challenge to Plato's Republic, and to the ideal Roman constitution of Polybius. For the Academic cyclic theory of history, Augustine offers the picture of two parallel lines which never meet, the one culminating in fire and the Judgment, the other in the vision of God. The Quest inaugurated in the *Confessions* on a more personal level is completed and fulfilled in the society of saints who together follow the celestial wisdom of the Gospel under the inspiration of God's victorious impulse, the grace of salvation.

An image that is constantly developed by St. Augustine throughout his works is that of Christ the Healer, the divine scapegoat in whose bruises we are redeemed. Indeed, throughout the New Testament, as many of the Fathers have suggested, there is a subtle connection between the physical cures which Christ performed and the supernatural healing which flowed from his redemptive mission. It was only fitting that Augustine should follow the primitive *kerygma* in its emphasis on the fourth Servant Song of Deutero-Isaias (*Is.* 53.1–12), in which Christ, the leper and the outcast, brings healing to all men. But Augustine develops the healing symbolism in quite a unique way. In one of his Sunday sermons (*Serm.* 87) he says:

> It is from sin, not from disease, that the human race suffers. Over the whole world, from east to west, the giant patient is stretched out. And to cure him the almighty Doctor must descend from heaven, humble Himself before mortal flesh, and, as it were, go to the bedside of His patient. . . . And yet the patient's powerful friends spurn Him, saying: "What an ignorant doctor!" . . . And does not this Doctor prove His skill by fulfilling all the promises? Destructive errors have been crushed throughout the world, and lustful desires have been repressed. . . . But do not say that the world was much better before; or that many terrible things have happened in the world since the divine Physician began to practice. Do not be surprised at this: even the operating room of a surgeon shows no trace of blood until he starts working on his patient . . . Go then to this Doctor, for now is the time to be healed.

Augustine develops the imagery in quite elaborate detail in the course of his works. Sin has entered the body of man like a poison, or infects him like a purulent wound. The divine Physician cures by contraries—urging humility and self-control, where the disease is caused by pride and self-indulgence. Only the patient who co-operates will be cured. Like the wise physician He must sometimes perform painful operations: cutting, burning, applying bitter remedies. But, if the medicine is bitter, says Augustine, Christ has first tasted it Himself in his Passion. This was the dramatization of our cure.

The culmination of Augustine's theological vision can be seen in the relationship between his doctrine of the image of God in man and his explanation of the mystery of the Trinity. His work *On the Trinity* comes from the last period of his productivity, and it is in the second part of the book that he develops the three analogies by which he sought to penetrate the great mystery. The first analogy is that of the three faculties of the soul, memory, intelligence, and will which spring from the same vital source and yet co-operate as distinct faculties in the work of salvation. The second analogy is that of the soul itself, which turns upon itself in self-knowledge, and through knowledge loves itself—as a symbol of the unity and trinity of God the Father, Son, and Holy Spirit. The last analogy takes the highest part of the soul, that which recalls the image of God (*memoria Dei*); the soul attempts to penetrate this image by understanding, and lastly comes to love God as a consequence of intelligence. These images have become classic in the history of Trinitarian theology.

Though they were for Augustine mere attempts, distant approximations of the awful mystery of the Godhead, their profound implication lies in the fact that man can begin to comprehend the Godhead precisely through the image of God that is within him. In Augustine the doctrine of the divine image in man has come full circle. For just as man betrayed the image within him by pride and disobedience, now he approaches the hidden veil of divinity precisely by the vestige of God imprinted on the human soul. Thus for Augustine the final mystery of the universe is the polarity between the Triune God and the image of God in the soul. And if man cannot fully understand God, neither can he be said fully to understand his own nature and his relationship to the Creator. Indeed, to understand God and the soul is the chief purpose of all philosophy (*Soliloquies* 1.2.7).

For Augustine, then, wisdom and love are the key to the mystery of the universe. God, whose Wisdom and Love expresses Itself in three Persons, communicates Himself through the cosmos under the veil of symbols and signs. His own image is impressed on man, the pinnacle of creation, in the faculties of knowledge and love. But man, created incorruptible, chose to follow the cupidity of the flesh rather than the attraction to divine love. And so Wisdom and Love becomes Incarnate, reconciles the enmities between God and man, and points the way to a new birth and restoration of the friendship which God had foreordained from the beginning of the world. Man now, through the painful process of conversion, using the light of the divine image impressed on his nature, must once again seek and find God—in the world, and through the Scriptures. But beneath the ciphers and mysteries, Truth remains ever one—the Wisdom and Love of God Who moves the world. Such is Augustine's system: it is through the image of God in man that the infinite abyss is somehow bridged. For Augustine true religion is, in part, the exploration of the universe. Thus in his theology there is an openness and clarity that is perhaps unique in all the Fathers of the Church. Christianity is not a mystery that is revealed to the few: it is a vision that brings ultimate understanding and peace. For, as he says in his eighty-eighth sermon on the Scriptures:

> The whole purpose is to restore to health the eye of the heart by which man can see God. . . . To this end is directed the entire aim of the holy Scriptures, that the inner vision may be cleansed of anything which keeps us from the sight of God.

Clarity and vision, therefore, form the ultimate purpose of his theology.

In breadth of imagery, in the richness of his sources, Augustine is perhaps the richest of all the Fathers of the Church. Though his mysticism is not of the same Oriental cast as that of Gregory of Nyssa, Augustine is indeed an ecstatic. Even in his fascination with science, music, and numbers he reveals the Plotinian influence. Most often, in his exegesis of the numbers of Scripture, he reflects not only Philonian allegory, but also a Pythagorean belief that numbers ultimately reflected the secret of the universe—and, in Augustine's case, the secrets of Christian revelation. The one hundred and fifty-three fish caught by the disciples in the miraculous draught is, for him, more than a merely vivid historical detail. In the 122nd homily on John, he offers the clue in the number 17: for 17 taken in arithmetical progression from 17 to 1 adds up to 153; and the number 17 symbolizes the total keeping of the Law (in the 10 commandments) and the seven gifts of the Spirit. Or, derived another way, 153 means the 3 of the Trinity plus 50 days before the coming of the Spirit, plus another fifty (which is arrived at by manipulating the number 7 again). Numbers are symbols of the formulae of the world; and, for Augustine, all the numbers of the Scriptures speak somehow of the works of God or the good deeds we must perform to attain Him. God is the ultimate source and clue for all the mathematical values of the universe.

It would be beyond our scope here to enter into a discussion of the works of Augustine. Suffice it to say that he raised Christian theology to new heights precisely because in his synthesis of Pauline Christianity and the allegorical-symbolic approach of

Alexandria he brought with him the philosophy and encyclopaedic knowledge of his age. What is so attractive about Augustine is his constant personal grappling with the revealed truths and intuitions of the Christian tradition, ever searching, ever willing to modify and change. In this he intimates the solution which we shall discuss in our final chapter.

The last stage in Augustine's development was in the period from the *City of God* to the *Retractations.* Now the technique of the *Soliloquies* has matured and given way to a more intuitive world-view. As he grew older, Augustine seems to have moved away from the symbolism of Neoplatonism, and to have insisted more and more on the centrality of Jesus' redemptive mission in his solution for the mystery of the soul's relationship to God. All throughout, however, is the concept of Wisdom as the specific virtue of the Christian teacher. Wisdom, though transmitted through words and signs, goes far beyond them; the deepest mysteries of grace and nature, God and the Atonement, cannot be expressed in the mere symbols of human language. Hence this wisdom must always be communicated and accepted with *Caritas,* love, in a humble spirit of faith. For it is not the mere communication of truth which transforms a man and moulds him in that higher life for which he was made. This enlightened wisdom is far more profound than the Platonic knowledge of the Ideas: it allows for the imperfections of man's darkness and inclination to evil; yet it assists him to see through his own inadequacies to the transcendent Reality beyond. By communicating His own Wisdom and Love through the world God will ultimately transform the *massa damnata,* "the accursed lump," into that *pleroma,* that fulfillment of Jesus which is the Church, the City of God, achieving its climax only in a life beyond the world. "In Him we live and move and are, yet we are not everywhere present as He is, while God is in man in His own unique way" (*Epist.* 187.10). Augustine's view of man profoundly foreshadows many of the insights of modern theology, and offers us the clue to the final dilemma posed by the imagination in Christian experience.

The Growth of Early Christian Poetry

CHAPTER SEVEN

THE BIRTH pangs of primitive Christian poetry were slow and painful. What poetic talent there was in the earliest days seems to have been devoted to rhythmic versions of the Biblical stories. Indeed, what further need was there of poetry if the means of salvation lay in the secrets of the Scriptures and in the catechetical voice of the Church? Even in the performance of the liturgy, the Church had taken over from the Synagogue the chanting of the psalms and the reading of other poetic books. Even here such poetry, whether read or chanted, was purely instructional or preparatory for the main liturgical act: the long Great Prayer of the Eucharist, wherein by the recitation of Christ's life and death the transformation of the bread and wine would be effected. It was natural then that original liturgical hymns would gain only slow admission into the Christians' services, and this usually under the aegis of a great name, as for example, Hilary, Ambrose, Gregory, and the like.

Two forces aided the rise of the liturgical hymn: first of all, the success of the Gnostic and heretical hymns; and secondly, the desire for personal expression with more concrete reference to the time and occasion for prayer. Thus it was that many of the earliest original hymns were those used at the celebration of the canonical hours; they could thus embody more explicit references to the Church and its worship than any of the psalms or canticles of the Old Testament. In this, it should be said, Ambrose and his circle were far superior to the heavy theological compositions of Hilary. The hymns of Ambrose were tautly composed, simple in their doctrine, and vivid in their imaginative projection of the Christian's needs.

It can be said that the heart of all Christian poetry is allegory. But it is the special sort of allegory developed by Origen and the Alexandrians out of the special midrashic techniques of Philo Judaeus. An illustration will make this clear. For the pagan poet, Quintilian tells us (*Institutes* 8.6.44 *ff.*), there were three kinds of allegory: the first was a continuous metaphor, such as illustrated by Horace's use of a ship for the party or the state; the second, the use of cover-names to designate historical characters or living people; and the third, the use of the riddling technique, in which the underlying reference must be deduced from clues. Horace in his *Epistles* (1.2) uses a sort of allegorical or moral interpretation of the poems of Homer, whereby the events portrayed refer to the passions of the human soul.

It was with some such technique in mind that Philo applied allegory to the Pentateuch: only here, as we have already seen, Philo's "enigma" or hidden meaning always referred to the special revelation of God for man, especially in the areas of moral philosophy, cosmology, and theology. Thus it was that the Alexandrians, in adapting the Philonian and, indeed, classical technique of allegorical interpretations, opened up a whole new dimension of theological speculation. However one may criticize them for their lack of evidential criteria in the interpretation of Scripture, it must be admitted that in allegory Christian poetry found at last a vehicle of expression and indefinite expansion. For now the images of daily life could become symbols of Christ and the Church, figures of the messianic era to come.

Still, in the earliest days it was difficult for any Christian poet to attempt a liturgical composition which would seem to rival the Psalms, which naturally formed the staple of the vigil service in the primitive Church. And yet, as the popularity of the Ambrosian hymns suggests, the Christians felt the need of a liturgical hymn which would more closely reflect their needs and beliefs, whose imagery would be more immediately grasped and understood. Nonetheless, the tonality and imagery of the Psalms had become so much a part of Christian life that it is almost impossible for us now to isolate their influence from the earliest Christian liturgical poetry. This is all the more strange in view of the distinctively Semitic motifs and symbols of the psalter.[26] For example, it is clear that different types of song tend to have a regularly recurrent motif. In the so-called Enthronement Songs (as *Psalms* 46, 92, 94–9, and many more), we see Iahweh enthroned in His Holy Place as King of the Jews and of all the nations; whereas in the cosmic hymns of thanksgiving and of praise, all creation is called on to render glory to the Lord of the heavens. In the more personal poems of affliction and lament, the psalmist speaks of himself as in an abyss of pain or despair, sometimes as physically ill or maltreated; and he calls upon the Lord to come as a shepherd, as a bulwark and fortress against his enemies and against the temptations that surround him. In the wisdom songs (as 1, 118, 111), the blessed are said to walk in justice and thus abide by the Law; they do not consort with the wicked or join in their impious rites. The lovely exile song (Psalm 136) pictures the Jews in Babylonia working on the canals and lamenting their sad lot: they have hung up their harps upon the poplars because they cannot sing to the Lord in a strange land. And the exiled priest or holy man of Psalm 42 bids Iahweh not to confuse him with the wicked and to restore him soon to Jerusalem, the Holy City.

This poignant, intense relationship between God and His people easily lent itself to development by the patristic writers and poets of the Christian period. The psalmist's depression, his sickness or physical distress, his affliction in a land of exile, was an appropriate symbol of fallen humanity awaiting the redemption, the raising up of all creation by the grace of Christ. The Jewish exile in Babylonia, and the work along the irrigation canals, became the exile of man from the Garden of Eden in a world of the wicked, awaiting the Final Coming of the Lord on the day of

[26] See the discussion in *Introduction à la Bible* by P. Auvray, I.585–621; for some of the relevant Akkadian and Ugaritic material on which the ancient psalmists drew, see J. B. Pritchard, *Ancient Near Eastern Texts Relating to the Old Testament* (2nd ed., Princeton, 1955).

Iahweh.[27] The hymns of praise and thanksgiving, on the other hand, that portrayed the mountains leaping for joy like sportive lambs, and all creation joining in harmony to the Lord, became songs of triumph over the victory of Jesus; and the Temple enthronement psalms would be applied to the entrance of the Lord into His glory.

Thus the prestige of the psalms in the liturgy has been longlasting. And yet the early Christians felt the need of something closer to their immediate experience.[28] The New Testament reflects this tendency in the hymns and canticles of the Gospels and Epistles, in the new song to the Lamb which is sung in the *Apocalypse*. Even the pagan Pliny wrote to Emperor Trajan (*Epistles* 10.96) that the Christians he had arrested "were wont to meet before dawn and sing a hymn to Christ as to a god." Thus the earliest Christian hymns were sung to Christ and to the Trinity, and only afterwards in honor of specific Christian mysteries. A lovely passage in Ignatius of Antioch (*Ephes.* 7.2) cites a hymn to Christ the divine Healer. In the East, however, the evidence suggests that the Gnostics were the first to develop liturgical hymns, and there is a stirring fragment quoted by Hippolytus of Rome. There are some hymn-like sections in Melito of Sardis' *Paschal Homily* dating perhaps from the second

[27] *Cf. St. Methodius: The Symposium* (American Christian Writers 27, Westminster, 1958), esp. pp. 76–80, 205–207, for the application of Psalm 136. There is a brief note on Psalm 136 and Psalm 44 in Auvray, *Introduction à la Bible,* I.609.

[28] On the growth of early Christian poetry, see Eleanor S. Duckett, *Latin Writers of the Fifth Century* (New York, 1930); for a treatment of both Latin and Greek, see the fine summary in Quasten, *Initiation aux Pères de l'Eglise,* I.179 *ff.* For the Latin world, see Raby, *A History of Christian-Latin Poetry;* and *cf.* also the relevant discussions in Christine Mohrmann, *Liturgical Latin: Its Origins and Character. Three Lectures* (Washington, D. C., 1957), esp. pp. 1–29 on the hieratic nature of Christian Latin; K. Strecker, *Introduction to Medieval Latin* (tr. and rev. by Robert B. Palmer, Berlin, 1957), esp. pp. 71 *ff.*, on mediaeval poetry; and W. Beare,, *Latin Verse and European Song: A Study in Accent and Rhythm* (London, 1957). For a number of stimulating comments, see Remy de Gourmont, *Le latin mystique: Les poètes de l'antiphonaire et la symbolique au moyen âge* (Paris, 1930).

century. And it is from the second century that we have the lovely Byzantine *Light Serene,* an evening-hymn to Jesus still preserved in the Greek Church:

> Now, O Jesus,
> At the hour of the dying sun,
> As we see the light of eventide appear
> We sing to Father, Son, and Spirit.

The same touching quality is preserved in the hymn which Clement of Alexandria quotes for us at the close of his treatise, the *Paedagogus,* or *Christians' Guide:*

> O King of the saints,
> Almighty Word of the Father, Lord most high,
> Sources and font of all wisdom,
> Comforter of sorrow,
> Lord of all time and space,
> Jesus, Savior of our race!

The famous Christian hymn found in a papyrus at Oxyrhynchus in 1922 is unique in that both words and musical notation have been preserved. The fragment, which goes back to the close of the third century or earlier, sings of the glory offered to the Triune God by the stars and the murmuring streams. Its orthodox Trinitarian theology perhaps reflects the widespread influence of Athanasius and the creed of Nicaea throughout the Egyptian Fayyum. The hymn incorporated in Methodius of Olympus' *Symposium on Chastity* (about 290) is an acrostic wedding song on the marriage of Christ and the Church and foreshadows the great *kontakia* or strophe-hymns of the early Middle Ages. Of Ephraem and Romanos, the great Oriental poets, we shall say more farther on.

St. Hilary of Poitiers (*d.* 367) was the first Father of the West to compose liturgical hymns, but it seems clear from the pieces and fragments that are preserved that they could never have become popular with the masses. But the hymns of St. Ambrose (*d.* 397) and his circle, predominantly in a classical iambic dimeter, wonderfully captured the spirit and imagery of the early liturgy. They formed the nucleus of the Milan hymnary, used there by clergy and consecrated men and women under Ambrose's stern guidance. Like the primitive Greek hymns of the East, Ambrose's austere pieces reflect the three levels of the Christian's life in time: the liturgical solemnity in the present recaptures the sacred history of salvation, and looks forward to the messianic banquet of the future life. Thus the Origenist triad, shadow-image-reality, was incorporated into the fiber of western liturgical poetry: the present life of the Church is an image of the reality to come, just as the types of the Old Law foreshadowed the sacramental fulfillment of all those who are baptized in the blood of the Lamb.

What is so fine about the Ambrosian hymns is their vigorous. lively imagery, often based on the canonical hours of prayer. Cock-crow brings the roseate dawn, the light of Christ, scattering the wicked and the works of darkness, heralding the Sun of justice and truth. The rising sun is a symbol of the Godhead and of Christ Himself, bringing warmth and vigor to men's bodies after the torpor of sleep. Sleep is the twin of death, and a symbol of sin. In the night come sinful fantasies, when wicked men do their work. Thus light and vigor stream from Jesus and the Church; the night shelters only the power of darkness. This Johannine imagery is deeply imbedded in the Ambrosian hymns and lends them, in their sprightly Latin rhythm, subtle charm and grace.

With Ambrose's imaginative genius and the stimulus of his monastic environment, the way was opened for a truly Christian poetry. And yet it is strange how rare it was yet to be. Part of the problem, as we have suggested, had to do with the value of poetry as such. But there was also the question of subject matter and technique. Ambrose's limited success tended to establish the pattern of poetic composition for many centuries: the Christian hymn would be composed for use in the canonical hours, or else in imitation of a liturgical hymn. Ambrose's prestige would, in a sense, stifle the growth of poetic achievement by the very act that gave it birth.

As for non-liturgical verse, the miracle is that it was produced at all. The young daughter of a Roman consul, Proba, who wrote Vergilian centoes on Biblical subjects, showed great courage (if neither talent nor originality). Then there were many Biblical hexameter poems, like the *Story of Sodom (De Sodom), Job,* and *Jonas (De Iona),* all of unknown authorship. The eighty poems which make up the two books of *Instructions,* written by the African Commodian about the time of the Decian persecution, were probably meant to be catecheses in verse. So too his *Apologetic Song (Carmen Apologeticum)* is a poetic version of the catechetic Narration: the story of God's dealings with man from the creation down to the Church, ending with the Last Things. Victorinus, an African rhetorician, wrote a poem on the Machabees and another on Easter, about the year 300. And two Spanish poets, who were to prepare the way for the great Prudentius, were Juvencus, a priest who composed a sort of Latin *Heliand,* or epic on the Saviour, about the time of Constantine; and Pope Damasus, whose epigrams on the martyrs have a rude sincerity, of more historic than poetic value.

Within the early Christian environment, the poetry of Prudentius, a Spaniard probably from Saragossa (349–*c.* 405), is quite remarkable.[29] We know about him hardly more than he tells us in his lyrical preface. A devoted civil servant all his life, now in his declining years he devotes himself to poetry as an act of divine homage and of prayer. The surprising fact is that so much of it is good. But in his *Martyrs' Crowns* and *Hymns for Daily Tasks (Cathemerion)* his model has been the canonical hymn, set for the different liturgical hours of the day and the various feasts of the year. They contain perhaps his most inspired work. The two theological treatises in verse, the *Apotheosis* (on the divinity of Christ) and the *Hamartigenia* (on the origin of sin and moral evil) are diletante theology, much as his *Reply to Symmachus* completed about 402–3, almost twenty years after Symmachus' attack, was ineffectual apologetic. Like much of Prudentius' lyric poems, the theological works were written, it would seem, merely to pass the time, or to afford entertainment

[29] On Prudentius, see Bernard M. Peebles, *The Poet Prudentius* (New York, 1951); Curtius, *European Literature and the Latin Middle Ages,* pp. 425 *ff.*; with the bibliography given in F. L. Cross, *The Oxford Dictionary of the Christian Church* (Oxford, 1957), p. 1119. Ernst Curtius tends to accept the view of Menéndez Pidal that Prudentius marks the beginning of a distinctively Spanish poetry.

for a restricted circle. His most ambitious work, and indeed the most popular during the Middle Ages, was the *Psychomachia,* the *Fight Over Man's Soul;* indeed, its strained allegories bore us perhaps as much as they delighted the mediaeval reader. Yet one suspects that so much of Prudentius is pure virtuosity: he boasts an enormous vocabulary range, a wide choice of subjects; but he lacks conciseness, order, or unified tone. This is why he can be pleasant in excerpts, but tedious when read in full. At times he can be, for a brief moment, quite charming, as in the two strophes of the 11th Hymn of the *Cathemerinon:* For The Nativity of Christ. They deal very touchingly with the young virgin Mother waiting for the birth of her babe (53–64):

Do you feel that burden like a flower
Growing chastely, maiden fair,
Towards birth's glorious hour
By God's maturing care?

All the world's joy behold
Within that virgin womb;
A new age, a light all gold
Emerges, as from a tomb.

The Babe's newborn cry
Brought the world a vernal breeze;
Reborn by His sigh
It shrugged off its dread disease.

But too often Prudentius' interest in the violent and the ghastly leads him into excesses. His portrait of John the Baptist nursed at his mother's shrunken breasts (*Cath.* 7.56 *ff.*) is perhaps no more than a *tour de force;* so too, the portrait of the corpses rising on the Last Day (*Cath.* 10.37 *ff.*). But his picture of Jonas passing through the mouth and gullet of the whale (*Cath.* 7.115 *ff.*) is nauseating; as is the description of the Holy Innocents with their "milky brains" being dashed on the ground (*Cath.* 12.117 *ff.*), and the raging and foaming of the madman of the Gospels (*Cath.* 9.52 *ff.*). His mastery of Latin and metric is a constant source of amazement; his extensive knowledge of pagan and Christian literature is quite outstanding for this period; but, when all is said, there is much that is simply not poetry. It is the rhetoric of the Spanish schoolroom, with its topics and figures, tropes and *colores;* there is the fervent apostrophe, the vivid *visio* (*hypotyposis,* as it was called in the schools), comparison (*synkrisis*), antithesis—but there is no imaginative transformation.

In the chaste quiet of his study, this aging Spanish official lavished his greatest efforts on scenes of violent bloodshed; and we see this not only in the poems on the martyrs, where there would have been reason perhaps, but also in the more philosophical *Fight Over Man's Soul.* In the tenth of the *Martyrs' Crowns* he gives us a unique picture of the Mithraic ceremony of taurobolium or bull-slaughter (*Perist.* 10.1010 *ff.*). Though the account is important for our knowledge of ancient religious cults, it is surprising that Prudentius saw fit to include it. In a sense, his picture of the priest of Mithras begrimed with clotted blood, drinking in the hot gore as it pours from the slain bull, is the most disgusting piece of verse in antiquity.

Blood-imagery is quite extensive in his poems. Blood flows all over Rome in a symbolic section of *Martyrs' Crowns* (11.45 *ff.*); and the faithful mop up the martyrs' blood from the ground in 11.135*ff.* The dumping of the living bodies of the great White Throng of martyrs into lime-pits is depicted in 13.76 *ff.* And the continuous violence and morbidity of the *Passion of the Virgin Eulalia* (*Crowns* 3) give it a prominence far beyond its merits. Eulalia steals out at the dead of night—not to a tryst, but to meet and taunt her executioners. There is a vivid description of the tearing of her young flesh, and the torture of the pyre. At the close there are the lovely crocuses, violets, and roses for her grave, which almost seem to symbolize the freshness and vitality which she renounced so early for her Lord. Its unity of tone is quite singular, but despite its power, so typical of Prudentius, it is not really more than a piece of sentimentalism. Prudentius surely reveals more talent than Ausonius, but his genius lacked direction and control. He did not appreciate the true problem of the Christian poet as did Paulinus; and worst of all, he did not know when to stop.

The Fight Over Man's Soul, or *Psychomachia,* is the first Christian allegory to be written in verse and its technique is to that extent most important. Actually Methodius' *Symposium* is a far more successful allegory in prose, but Prudentius' characterization of the Virtues and Vices was to have an important influence on mediaeval genres. He takes the lists of Virtues inherited from Paul and clothes them in the manner of the *Apocalypse* or the *Shepherd* of Hermas. The first stage of the battle over man's salvation is clearly conceived: there are single combats, prefaced by debates in the manner of the epic writers, between Faith and Idolatry, Chastity and Lust, Patience and Anger, Humility and Pride. Again the poet scatters on the canvas his most brilliant rhetorical colors. Chastity (*Pudicitia*) is attacked by Lust (*Libido sodomitica*), who tries to blind the young virgin with a sulphurous torch. Lust is overwhelmed, and after a long speech on the Christian conquest of the flesh, she is condemned to the Abyss. The battle becomes confused when hordes of handmaidens join it on both sides, Fasting, Jesting, Charm, Sobriety, and so on. The climax comes when Discord, or Heresy, tries to stab the virgin Concord with a dagger; at this point Faith steps in and handily subdues the female warrior. In a typically Prudentian ending, all the good Ladies come forward and brutally tear apart the body of Heresy limb from limb, scattering the pieces to animals and birds. Then a new edifice is built to Christ, in which Wisdom sits enthroned amid blossoming roses and lilies.

If Prudentius was the greatest Christian poet of this early period, he indeed poses a problem. His vividness too often seems like a rhetorical striving for effect; his emotion, insincere and excessive. Much of it reminds us, in its own way, of the pedantic closet-verse of Gregory of Nazianzus, though Prudentius was far more conscientious an artist. But even though Prudentius' verse seems far more objective than Gregory's turgid *To Myself*, it nonetheless represents his own violent struggles, his own conflicts, his own search for a vision. Perhaps the center of all his poetry may be found in the closing apotheosis of the *Passion of Agnes* (*Crowns* 14). As the executioner's sword has cut through her neck, her virgin soul rises high above the earth (14.91 *ff.*); now at last she sees the cosmos as it really is:

> The twisting and turning of the world,
> The life lived within a black whirlwind;

and all the petty vanities that men live for; she sees

> The long sorrows and all too brief joys,
> The smouldering brands of men's spite,
> And the dark clouds of heresy.

Agnes then grinds the serpent's head with her heel as he spits out his venom; and she is at last received into Paradise. It is a vision that recalls Perpetua's in the *Passion* attributed to Tertullian; the apotheosis motif had many pagan forebears, as we have seen; but in Prudentius it becomes perhaps his most inspired passage, enshrining as it does his own authentic vision.

Two poets of the latter part of the fourth century should be taken together, Ausonius of Bordeaux (consul in A.D. 379) and his poetic "son" or protegé, Paulinus of Nola.[30] A world of difference separated both their talents and their Christianity. Ausonius was the pedantic schoolmaster, his head full of quotations in place of ideas. His poetry was metrically precise but, with the exception of a few short passages, lacking either beauty or inspiration. The wonder is that Ausonius himself never seems to have realized it. Paulinus, on the other hand, educated at Bordeaux and destined for the civil service, became with his pious wife Therasia the center of a sturdy monastic revival in Campania. He wrote far less, but what he did was endowed with his own authentic Christian vision; he wrote from the heart, and not from books. And though all of Paulinus is not equally good, what there is breathes a depth of awareness and a sense of the growing conflict between art and Christianity. The two poetic letters he wrote to Ausonius (*carm.* 10 and 11) have become a kind of *Ars poetica christiana.* Ausonius' greatest achievement was perhaps to have been the tutor of Paulinus.

Ausonius seems to have taken the view that Paulinus' devoted

[30] On Ausonius and Paulinus a vast amount has been written: see the summary bibliographies in Cross, p. 110 (Ausonius), and 1035–36 (Paulinus of Nola). See also Raby, *A History of Christian-Latin Poetry,* pp. 101 *ff.*; and his other volumes, *A History of Secular Latin Poetry* (2 vols., Oxford, 1934), 1.54–65. On Paulinus *cf.* also Nora K. Chadwick, *Poetry and Letters in Early Christian Gaul* (London, 1955), pp. 63–88.

wife Therasia gained such an ascendency over him that he was drawn away from the carefree, worldly life which Ausonius obviously enjoyed. It is only natural to suppose that Ausonius' Christianity was barely skindeep: where he does express himself on heaven and the deity he seems far more pagan than Christian. As for his verse—it seems incredible that such a prolific writer could not have found more to say. Perhaps his best lines may be found in his song of the river, *Moselle;* here he allows what is obviously sincere sentiment to break through the crust of tasteless pedantry. But the vision of the vine-laden banks reflected in the glassy waters is soon destroyed by mythological lore and a catalogue of fish. Even in what seems to have been his masterpiece, Ausonius is more interested in parading his useless knowledge than in sustaining an impression of beauty. By the time we come to the final impassioned apostrophe to the Moselle, "mother of men and of fruit," the poet has lost us and we regret that we have read him so far. Even his illicit love for the little German Mädchen Bissula, whom he met while on campaign in the Alamannic War about the year 371, finds him unequal to the task of poetic expression. What Horace or even Tibullus would have made of Bissula!

Ausonius' finest complete poem is the brief elegy (*Epigram* 40) to his wife, written a few years before she was to die in A.D. 343. Ausonius was only thirty-three at her death, and hence it is incorrect to refer to the poem, as some have done, as though it were written in his old age. It is, however, a wish that their love may never grow old:

> Dear love, let us live as we always have
> And keep the pet-names we gave each other
> In our first love. Let no day ever change
> Each other in our eyes: I shall always be
> Your young man, and you my little girl.
> And even though I may grow as old as Nestor,
> And you as shrivelled as the Cumaean Sibyl,
> We shall always forget what old age is
> And count its merits, never, never its years.

However trivial the thought and trite the language, this eight-line elegy is perhaps Ausonius' most lasting work. If the poem had been longer, he could not have resisted the impulse to make it pedantic or rhetorical.

But of all the tasteless pieces on which Ausonius squandered his talent, the most outrageous is the *Marriage Cento* or hotchpotch of lines taken from Vergil's works and dedicated to his friend Paulus about the year 368. The account of a fictional wedding, it remains one of the most obscene poems of the ancient world—a "literary outrage," indeed, as one scholar has called it. Ausonius' description of it, in the covering dedication to Paulus, is a fitting summary of a good deal of Ausonius' poetry: *frivolum et nullius pretii opusculum,* which is excellent Latin for "a giddy and completely worthless piece of work."

It is curious that such opposite characters as Ausonius and Paulinus should have both arisen from the same milieu at Bordeaux, Ausonius' poetic letters to his pupil seem to fall during the years when Paulinus, now baptized, was in Spain with his wife (A.D. 389–394) up until the death of their long desired child. In 394, after Paulinus was ordained at Barcelona, they emigrated to Italy and settled at Nola in Campania, where Paulinus became the guardian of the tomb and shrine of St. Felix, a local Italian saint; and both he and his wife became the center of a thriving monastic community. Paulinus is one of the most charming figures of the early Church.

At any rate, we are grateful to Ausonius for having elicited by his poetic epistles (23–29) some of Paulinus' finest pieces. Ausonius berates him for his piety, and almost seems to want Paulinus to leave his wife, that domineering "Tanaquil" as he calls her, a pedantic reference to the wife of the Roman king Tarquinius. Ausonius wrote four letters, only three of which reached Paulinus, all together, in the year 393, the year of his ordination at Barcelona; of these only two apparently are extant, *Epist.* 28, 29. Paulinus replied in what we now have as *Epist.* 31, his most important work. In 393 Ausonius wrote once again (*Epist.* 27), and received a more kindly reply (*Epist.* 30). With this the correspondence came to a close: Ausonius was already over eighty years old, and Paulinus, now a priest, was ready to embark on a new life in Italy. Paulinus' famous reply, *Epist.* 31, is the classic Christian statement of the dilemma between art and religion, even though its occasional sharp tone was evoked by Ausonius' teasing raillery. It is truly a Christian Art of Poetry, at once breathing a deep spirituality in its attempt to express Paulinus' supernatural ideals to the worldly, sensuous Ausonius. After a very short introduction on the delay of the letters (in elegiacs), Paulinus picks up the main theme in a long series of iambics (*Epist.* 31.19–102). Here occur the decisive words:

> You urge me, Master, to take up again
> The Muses I have long abandoned. But why?
> Hearts pledged to Christ are closed to Apollo,
> And deny entrance to the goddesses of song.
> Once we worked as equals in zeal if not in power,
> To drive the deaf Apollo from his Delphic cave,
> To invoke the divine Muses, and drink from groves
> And hills the gift of utterance from the gods.
> But now another force, a greater God urges me,
> Demanding another way of life, claiming the gift
> He Himself gave, that we may live for His Father.

Life now, says Paulinus, is a yoking of God and man in constant conversation (55–6). Christ's message has shown us the true value of earthly life, and of the childish passions which absorb so much of our time. Now, by faith and hope the Christian acquires a new form of perception: *secreta ignitus penetrans caelestia sensus* (173), "a fiery sense that pierces the secrets of heaven." For Ausonius' gibes have at last brought out Paulinus' clear awareness of his Christianity (174 *ff.*):

> For what the eye sees is but passing;
> Invisible are the things that are eternal,
> Glimpsed only in spirit and embraced by hope.

Ausonius' criticisms are, then, ill-timed; Paulinus is doing merely what he wants to do—now that he has realized (288 *ff.*)

> Man is a slender thing, of sickly body
> And passing season, and—without Christ—
> Shadow and dust.

Paulinus has prayed that he may be able to rise with ease at the Final Coming, and that the world's fetters will not hold him back from rising high into the heavens with Christ to join the blessed there (306 *ff.*). His vision of the Last Day foreshadows the *Dies Irae.* In the final letter of the correspondence (*Epist.* 30) Paulinus adopts an even kindlier tone. "Never shall I live apart from you in spirit," he writes;

> Even when I am released from the body's prison
> And have flown from this earth, wherever the Father
> May place me, there will I bear you in my heart.
> . . . Farewell, beloved Master.

If Paulinus' calm strikes us as sometimes colorless, it is because he is afraid of the tricks of the old school. His message is straight and plain; the song of birds and the sweep of wings are his most common image. Prudentius showed a more secure grasp of poetic diction and the tautness of direct vision; but surely no other poet had a more profound awareness of the role of the Christian artist than Paulinus. And no other early poet has given it clearer expression.

The feast of St. Felix was held on Jan. 14, in the midst of the Italian winter; but Paulinus suggests that it brought a spiritual spring to all believers—a spring that proclaimed the death of the old gods and the resurrection of Jesus. It is difficult to do justice to Paulinus' charming verses on the spring-in-winter of the festival of St. Felix:

> Bird's song heralds the spring: so my voice
> Has its spring in Felix's feast, in whose light
> Men make merry and—ah!—even winter flowers.
> Without, there's still the gloomy cold and the year
> Drags amid hoar and frost, with the earth hard
> Under its shroud of white. Still our pious joy
> On our patron's feast makes the spring, and banishes
> Winter in the soul, dispels the fog of sadness
> And leaves the heart serene.

Just as the swallows know the change of the seasons and fly back into the orchards with the other birds, singing a new song with glistening wings, he continues,

> So I too know the day that the year brings back
> To pay due honor to Felix. I know when spring

Is reborn again, and when it is time to sing
A new song in token of my renewed prayer.

The celebration of Felix's feast as a spring-in-winter suggests the banishment of the darkness, the cold of sin and spiritual death usually associated with the winter season. For spring is the time of rebirth, the season of resurrection. In Paulinus there is a delicate fusion of the old pagan pastoral motifs and the joy of Christianity. The Muses are cast out, but the nightingale still celebrates the dawn and the woods blossom with flowers of deeper hue.

One thing Paulinus did was to establish a sharply focussed Christian approach to the marriage-hymn, especially in his *Epithalamium for Julianus,* whose spouse was a Christian lady named Titia. It is a refreshing change from the vulgar innuendoes of the Roman Hymen-song, even in such charming hands as those of Catullus. For all that, however, Paulinus is quite Roman: he emphasizes the old moral notion of the *castum foedus* or bond of fidelity between the lawfully married, such as we also find it reflected in the inscription called *In Praise of Turia,* a pagan eulogy of a good wife from the Augustan age. In this brief, lovely elegy, Paulinus begs Christ to join the two virginal souls as two doves under his yoke. The symbolism of the yoke of virgins blends into the yoke of Christ; for this, after all, is the meaning of the union of Julianus and Titia in purity and piety.

Banish from their bed all vulgarity:
Juno, Cupid, Venus—and all their luxury!

It is a plea that the older Roman marriage mores return; now, however, they are sanctioned by the "priest's holy pact" as the Church's final seal upon what is best in man and women. Gregory of Nazianzus' *Epithalamium for Olympias,* the lovely young woman who was to be deaconess of Constantinople under Chrysostom, is hardly poetry, and in any case expresses the monastic view of the married state; it has at times the quality of a lamentation. But Paulinus, whose wife Therasia meant so much to his faith, has a more authentically Christian concept of marriage. The gentle purity of lyric is typical of Paulinus; it is quite the opposite pole to the childish prurience of Ausonius'

Marriage Cento. Unfortunately we do not find its equal till the student songs and Franciscan hymns of the Middle Ages.

Ausonius and Paulinus present a strange dichotomy within the poetic awareness of the early Church: Ausonius, the rhetorician, whose Christianity has hardly penetrated his imagination or his understanding; Paulinus, the talented and energetic churchman whose deep piety did not stifle his artistic achievement, but rather, if anything, enhanced it. Paulinus' fusion of the sensuous image with a deep experience of Christian conversion produces a poetry which is both moving and authentic. Though lacking the broad, garish canvas of Prudentius, he is superior to him in calm depth and purpose. A combination of Paulinus' Christian vision and Prudentius' virtuosity would have produced a greater poet perhaps than any that arose from the Roman empire.

The Rise of Monastic Poetry

CHAPTER EIGHT

THE GREAT poetry of monastic spirituality was only the culmination of a broad stream of poetic catechesis, much of it thin and lacking in either talent or inspiration. As early as the year 300 there circulated an anonymous poem entitled *The Tree of Life,* once attributed to St. Cyprian of Carthage. Surely African, and impregnated with Alexandrian ideas, it inaugurated the elaborate tree-imagery which became classic with the poems of Venantius Fortunatus and Bonaventure. *The Tree of Life* is an early form of poetic catechesis, a narrative of the life and death of Christ. The same technique is used by Marius Victor of Marseilles (*d.* 426) in his miniature epic on truth entitled *Alethias* (probably incomplete), recounting the history of salvation from Genesis down to the destruction of Sodom. Dracontius' hexameters on *The Praises of God* about the year 500 summarize the catechetical narrative from a more philosophical point of view.

Among the best of the poets of this dreary period was Caelius Sedulius, born, perhaps at Rome, in the early part of the fifth century. In his *Carmen Paschale* or *Easter Song* dedicated to Macedonius, the author, as it were, of his conversion to Christianity, he attempts to rival the work of the earlier Juvencus by resuming the Old and New Testaments in epic form, to which he later appended a prose summary entitled *Opus Paschale.* Despite the archaic flavor due to classical and Vergilian phrases, Sedulius' verse is somewhat crude and heavy but not entirely uninspired. He is among the first poetically to exploit the imagery of the Virgin Mother and the mysteries of Christ's birth. In his so-called *Acrostic Paean for Christ's Nativity* he summarizes the mysteries of the holy Childhood: each stanza begins with a new letter of the alphabet in order, a common device derived from Hebrew poetry and often used to symbolize perfection, totality, and unity. Some of his best lines on the Virgin Mary were adapted for some of the Marian Masses of the Roman liturgy:

> Hail, mother truly blest for having born a King!
> For He reigns over earth and heaven; His might
> And power, all-encompassing, abide
> Forever. She, whose joy it was to bear
> Her God in her blessed body, had no peer
> Either in our first mother or in all women
> Who were to come. But alone of all her sex
> She pleased the Lord. O Christ, hear our prayer—
> For to the dead world You gave life by living there.

For all the faults of the *Paschal Song* it surpasses most of the dull catecheses that emerged from the Patristic period.

Avitus, Bishop of Vienne (*c.* 450–525), wrote five books of hexameters on the Old Testament history from Adam to Moses. Orientius, who was perhaps bishop of Autun about the middle of the fifth century, wrote a *Commonitorium* or *Manual of Moral Guidance,* and his catechesis, though it deals with the life of Jesus and the Last Things, has a rather unique discussion of the virtues and vices in elegiac distichs.

Three interesting anonymous poems should be mentioned here, *On the Phoenix* from about the year 300; *A Husband to His Wife,* a fifth century piece; and *On the Day of Judgment,* perhaps from the sixth or the seventh. The last-named hymn is typical of many Judgment poems, anticipating the idea, but hardly the fire, of the *Dies Irae.* The poetic address of *A Husband to His Wife* is a mild piece in the spirit of Paul's first letter to the Corinthians: "those that have wives should be as though they had none." But the most fascinating of these curious verses is the fantastic *De Ave*

Phoenice, On the Phoenix.[31] The symbolism of the phoenix—apparently a type of heron—with its suggestion of the rising sun and the eternal renewal of life—could have been adapted by a Christian, but the tacit approval of sun-worship seems to suggest pagan authorship. Clement of Rome, as we have seen, did use the symbol as a token of God's promise of immortality, and much later the Italian philosopher Giordano Bruno (*d.* 1600) wrote a poem to the Phoenix in which he makes it a symbol of the ever-recurrent life force of the universe. But the treatment here, however, can only by a stretch of the imagination be called Christian; hence some scholars have attributed it to Lactantius in the period before his conversion, following a suggestion of Gregory of Tours. The poem fascinated the Middle Ages, and the Old English poem *The Phoenix* is a derivative work. Actually the Old English piece, only the first 380 lines of which are based on the Latin *Phoenix,* is the superior work; obviously written by a learned Angle about the time of Cynewulf (about A.D. 900)—who has by some been thought to be its author—the Anglo-Saxon poem develops the allegorical meaning of the phoenix as a symbol of Christ and the elect. By comparison the Latin poem seems a rhetorical exercise, of the sort we would expect from Ausonius, Ennodius, or Sidonius Apollinaris.

Boethius and Venantius Fortunatus herald, each in his own way, the coming of the Middle Ages. Though not strictly a poet, Boethius loved to insert lines of verse in the text of his *Consolation of Philosophy,*[32] and much of it breathes the same gentle Platonic air. The immortal vision of the Lady Philosophy, who comes to comfort him within the dungeons of Theodoric, anticipate Dante's

[31] See Raby, *A History of Christian-Latin Poetry,* p. 15; B. Altaner, *Patrologie* (Freiburg, 1950), pp. 153 *ff.*; Quasten, *Patrology* (Westminster, 1953), II.403–404). On the whole, Quasten would seem to favor Lactantius' authorship of the poem.

[32] On Boethius, see P. de Labriolle, *History and Literature of Christianity from Tertullian to Boethius* (tr. H. Wilson, New York, 1925), pp. 409–505; Helen M. Barrett, *Boethius: Some Aspects of His Times and Work* (Cambridge University Press, 1940); Curtius, *European Literature and the Latin Middle Ages,* esp. pp. 102–105, and *passim;* Gilson, *History of Christian Philosophy,* pp. 97–106 with the notes.

Beatrice; and there is a quiet nostalgia in the welcome bits of verse (V, metre 3):

> What caused the strife of the world?
> What god made the split between Truth
> And Truth that never can be joined?
> Or is Truth really one,
> And the soul oppressed with the weight
> Of flesh cannot glimpse the links
> By the light of its stifled fire?

The lady Philosophy offers the aging Boethius "stronger remedies" than he has had before. She bids him consider the brevity of man's life; in comparison with eternity and the immortality of the soul all human honors are worthless (II, metre 7):

> Though glory carries your name
> To many climes, and your household
> Glories in its noble rank,
> Yet Death scorns reputation
> And buries both great and small.

The text of the *Consolation* thus rambles between prose and verse like the ancient pagan Menippean satire; and, though most often abstract, the poetic summaries of the prose dialogues are as good as anything written during the period. Boethius' quest for a Christian counterpart to the Platonic solution lends his verse a sharp purpose and a serious direction—"the light of its stifled fire"—something so many contemporary poets lacked. At the end of book three (metre 9), he prays:

> Grant, my God, that my mind may rise
> To see Thy solemn throne, to glimpse
> The fount of Good, to see Thy face
> With new vision. Dispel the fog of earth,
> The weight of the flesh, and send forth lightning
> In Thy glory. Thou art the peace, the rest
> Of the soul. To see Thee is our end,
> And our beginning: in Thee the guide,
> Path, pilgrim, goal, are all in one.

Whether the *Consolation* is a documentary record of a conflict or the presentation of a solution is not easy to say. Boethius is struggling in the face of Death for a vision, a reconciliation between the philosophy he believed in all his life and the harsh realities of final annihilation. Though the mother-figure that appears to him bears upon her dress the symbols of philosophy, it is to Neo-Platonism that Boethius ultimately has recourse. The Father on whom he calls for light rather resembles Plotinus's One; there is no reference to Christ, the Atonement, a sacramental Church. Redemption in the end is achieved by vision and fortitude; and the final stage of Philosophy's revelation is a cold, starry portrait of the eternal, all-seeing God, in Whose sight man is obliged to live righteously: "Great is the necessity of living a good life, if you would not deceive yourselves; for all your acts lie open before the eyes of the Judge Who sees all things" (V.48). Poetically this is more beautifully expressed at the close of book four (IV, metre 7):

Heaven is the crown of labor.
Stout hearts, walk where the road
Of courage leads. Don't yield!
Don't falter or turn back!
Earth conquered gains the stars.

If the *Consolation* is indeed the record of a soul in torment rather than, like Dante's *Commedia,* the gage of victory achieved, it represents nonetheless Platonism's last bequest to the dawning Middle Ages.

A most welcome figure during the waning decades of the sixth century is Venantius Fortunatus (540–600),[33] a wandering scholar of private means, born at Treviso and educated at Ravenna. At about the age of twenty-five, when most young blades were courting their ladies, Venantius set off for Gaul to thank his saintly patron, Martin of Tours, for curing his eyes. He visited many cities of Germany and Gaul before he ended his pilgrimage at Tours, and then at last arrived at Poitiers. There he was given

[33] On Venantius, *cf.* W. Kroll and F. Skutsch, *W. S. Teuffels Geschichte der römischen Literatur* (ed. 6, 3 vols., Berlin, 1913), III.523–38; Raby, *A History of Secular Latin Poetry,* I.127–42; Curtius, *op. cit.,* pp. 160 *f.,* 411 *f.*; Ladner, *The Idea of Reform,* p. 423 (Venantius' idea of friendship). *Cf.* also Beare, *Latin Verse and European Song.* *pp.* 261 *f.;* Remy de Gourmont, *Le latin mystique,* pp. 90 *ff.*

shelter at the famous monastery founded by Queen Radegunde, the Thuringian princess who had been forced to marry the brutal Lothar I. Lothar, in addition to murdering her brother, proved a difficult and exacting husband; among other things, Venantius tells us, he did not relish his wife's austerities and nightly vigils. At length she ran off, and with a young girl named Agnes founded the Convent of the Holy Rood at Poitiers under the Rule for Women written by Caesarius of Arles. Thanks to Venantius and to Gregory of Tours, the convent is one of the best documented of the early middle ages. An austerity even more severe than the Lady Radegunde's would have softened at the sight of the friendly poet-wanderer Venantius, and in return for the nuns' friendship he composed hymns, poetic letters, and *vers d'occasion* to brighten their lives. To the semi-barbaric society of Poitiers, the young Italian from Ravenna brought the breath of the old classical culture, the spirit of Horace, Catullus, and Vergil.

But what is most striking in all his writings is the atmosphere of Christian friendship and love. Venantius is bound to all his friends, clerical, religious, and lay, in a wonderful aura of sweetness; even though far away, he is always united to them by the Spirit of Love, that Spirit that binds all those who are stamped in His image just as, in a sense, it binds the Persons of the Godhead. Indeed, as we read between the lines of the *Life of Radegunde* which Venantius wrote, we can detect a touch of mediaeval courtly love in the poet's devotion to her, and in the friendship and lavish hospitality she offered him. In this idyllic atmosphere he remained, happily writing his verses until Radegunde's death some twenty years later. He himself took orders and then, after another period of wandering, finally returned to Poitiers to become its bishop, staying there until his death. By this time, as Gregory of Tours tells us, the monastery of the Holy Rood had become a scandal in the lack of discipline of its nuns under the successor of the saintly Radegunde.

Venantius' attractive and childlike personality is reflected in the poetry and hymns he wrote for Queen Radegunde, for the Abbess Agnes, and their circle; indeed, his poetic talent blossomed under the care and affection that was showered on him at Holy Rood. Not since Paulinus of Nola was there such a delicate fusion of classic style with deeply felt Christianity. In a more serious moment, a hymn to the Abbess Agnes praises the virgin's body as the very bridal chamber of the Word (*Opera* VIII.3). Yet, in a gayer mood, he praises the delectable gifts the nuns showered on him. Dishes are piled "hill-high" with meat and other dainties; there are vegetables and fruit on marble salvers, apples in baskets, milk in black jars, lots of rich cream, plums and eggs, fine goose and wine. Food-descriptions for Venantius become the vehicle of his joy and good spirits, his love for all these good people in the Lord. He chides himself on eating too much and dozing after a heavy meal. In return he will send the Lady Radegunde a simple bunch of violets or a basket of ripe plums. There is a fine, rich sensuousness here that will perhaps remind one of Keats.

But his imagination was especially fired by the image of the Cross; and when the emperor Justin II and his wife Sophia sent Radegunde a fragment of the true Cross to be reserved at Poitiers, Venantius composed three of his greatest pieces, the *Vexilla regis* (*The King's Standard*), *Crux benedicta* (*The Blessed Rood*), and *Pange lingua* (*Sing, My Tongue*). The occasion is one of the best known in the history of the early Church, preserved for us in the pages of Gregory of Tours' *History of the Franks.* Gregory was particularly interested in the later problems which the monastery caused after Radegunde's death; and in connection with the relationship which the convent had with the bishops, he tells us (*History* 9.40) that it was the bishop of Tours, and not of Poitiers, who came with his clergy to the monastery in 569 to bring the sacred relics at Radegunde's request, "with much chaunting of psalms, with the splendor of lighted candles and incense." It was for this festival, then, that the young Venantius composed his great hymns.

The central idea of the *Vexilla regis* (II.6 in his collected works) is taken from the Old Latin version of Psalm 95.10: "Tell the people that the Lord has reigned from the wood." This mistranslation was corrected by Jerome in his second revision, the so-called Gallican psalter, and the usual modern version of this enthronement hymn reads: "Tell it among the people: the Lord reigns." Thus in the poem, Venantius' central image is of the Cross as a rude wooden throne, dyed with royal purple; then it becomes a Paradise-tree laden with precious fruit, and exuding perfume from its bark. This poem is not as unified nor so sharply focussed as the great *Pange lingua.*

In his second poem on the Cross, *Crux benedicta* (*Opera* II.1), Venantius stresses the symbolism of the Cross as a tree. It is planted in a luxurious orchard, the source of fertility and life, by the waters of life and grace. Its fruit and leaves are bright and luscious; and at its magic odor even the dead come to life. Though perhaps not so well known as the other two poems, its imagery is strikingly beautiful and recalls the descriptions of the Elysian fields which we find in the earlier poets of the classical period.

But of all Venantius' vast and staggering output, there is no piece more justly admired than the *Pange lingua* (II.2). Here the stream of Christian tradition has surely swelled the poet's imagination. Even Ephraem, the Syriac poet of the fourth century, for all his sturdy imagery of Christ as the intrepid sailor bringing his wooden bark home to harbor (*Hymn on the Church and Virginity* 31), cannot surpass the clear craftsmanship of Venantius. It is, in small compass, a summary of the Christian doctrine of the Atonement. If we may translate the stirring opening verses:

Sing, my tongue, the laurels of that wondrous strife,
Sing a song of triumph on the trophy of the Cross
Tell the way the world's redeemer by His sacrifice brought life.

When our Maker sorrowed at our parents' fatal bite,
He marked down the deadly tree that had been the sinful source
And determined it should save us from our long and painful plight.

And the lovely closing verses:

Bend your branches, lofty Tree, and relax that sacred side;
Soften the rude harshness that you received at birth,
And to a soft and easy bed the High King's limbs confide.

Alone were you judged worthy to be the Victim's rood,
And bring, as an ark to harbor, the tossing shipwrecked earth.

Caulked against the sea waves by the Lamb's own sacred
Blood.

Adapting the trochaic tetrameter of the legionary's marching songs, Venantius has caught the secret of the authentic Christian hymn, with its three levels: the messianic past, the liturgical present, and the eschatological future, corresponding to the three stages in the growth of the Church in time.

The *Pange lingua* is Venantius' greatest achievement. The Cross stands like a Roman army's trophy recalling the victory of salvation; for the same tree that had offered our first parents the fatal fruit was marked by God for man's redemption. Venantius follows the old legend that Adam brought a branch of the Tree of Knowledge out of Paradise and that it was planted and grew again. The symbol of the Paradise-tree recurs in the art of the catacombs and the early Church: the Cross is a flowering tree that offers solace to the birds of the air.

It is the symbol of wood (*lignum*) that binds the imagery together. After a touching picture of Jesus bound in swaddling bands within a narrow crib, we see the Saviour raised up as a sacrificial Lamb upon the Tree. Now the Tree, the fairest in all the world, flowers; and as the imagery softens, the poet begs the tree to become soft and yielding under the body of the Redeemer. And just as the blood became a stream to wash the entire universe, so now he sees the wood as a raft carrying the "price of the world," bringing the shipwrecked world to harbor. It is a remarkably taut piece of work; in it the tension of time and eternity have reached a calm focus in the Cross of Jesus, caulked against the storms of the world by the blood of the scapegoat lamb.

In addition to Alcuin of York, the Court of Charles the Great boasted of three poets of some merit, Paul the Deacon, Paulinus of Aquileia, and Theodulf of Orleans. Alcuin wrote correct but unremarkable verse; though he called himself Flaccus, it is clear that his talents lay elsewhere. Alcuin's dialogues with Charles *On Dialectic* and *On Rhetoric and the Virtues* constitute his doctrine on poetry and rhetoric; but in their stress on the tropes and figures as the clue to poetry they only served to keep alive a false concept of the creative imagination. In any case it is interesting to note that even the charming pastoral, *The Strife between Winter and Spring,* attributed by many to Alcuin, seems certainly not by him. Here young Daphnis and old Palaemon are referees in a pastoral singing match between Winter and Spring that recalls the atmosphere of Vergil's *Eclogues.* The constant mention of the *cuculus,* the cuckoo, comes as a refrain, and the pagan spring imagery has a quiet nostalgic air. It is a slight work, but surely better than anything else in Alcuin's poetic corpus.

Paul the Deacon was a Lombard of noble family (730–*c.*799) and is best known for his *History of the Lombards.* His vast learning in both Latin and Greek and his efficient Latin style did not, however, make him a poet. His famous set of sapphic strophes in imitation of Horace on the Feast of John the Baptist are well-known because of its first stanza:

> *Ut* queant laxis *re*sonare fibris
> *mi*ra gestorum *fa*muli tuorum
> *sol*ve polluti *la*bii reatum
> *s*ancte *I*oannes;

the marked syllables were adapted by Guido of Arezzo to produce the names of the notes of his musical scale. But as Latin verse it is an exercise in school rhetoric, stilted and artificial. This is not to suggest that Paul was untalented: we catch a glimpse of Catullan inspiration in the lovely lines he wrote on Lake Como, and in the pathetic epitaph for a little girl who died in childhood. His imagination, however, is seen at its best in the tales he recounts in the *History of the Lombards,* as, for example, the story of the miraculous bodies of the Seven Holy Sleepers.

Paulinus, a grammarian at the court of Charles, was made patriarch of Aquileia in the year 787. We are unsure of the attribution of much of his poetry, but I should like to think that he composed the lovely hymn, *Ubi caritas et amor ibi Deus est,* on the occasion of the Synod of Friuli on the border of modern Jugoslavia. For the performance of the Maundy ritual of Holy Thursday the Roman Missal has adapted some of the stanzas of Paulinus' hymn.[34]

[34] See F. J. E. Raby, *The Oxford Book of Medieval Latin Verse* (Oxford, 1959), pp. 76–77, with note.

Our bond of union is Christ's love:
Have joy, be glad in Him.
We must both love and fear the Lord,
Love Him with all our heart.
Ubi caritas et amor, ibi Deus est. . . .

Once met together
Let nothing divide us in spirit,
No mean quarrel or cavil:
Then will Christ be in our midst.
Ubi caritas et amor, ibi Deus est.

Indeed, "Where There is Love, There is God" recalls, in its simple piety, the spiritual vigor of an earlier age. Though once thought to have been a Benedictine hymn composed for the weekly Maundy, or washing of feet, more informed studies have now restored it to Paulinus.

Another poet who graced the Caroline court was Theodulf (*d.* 821),[35] a scholar of Spanish-Gothic origin who was consecrated bishop of Orleans in 798. Intelligent, well-read in Christian and pagan Latin literature—Alcuin called him the Pindar of the circle—his wit got him into the black books of Louis the Pious and he was condemned to a dungeon at Angers in 818. The vast bulk of his work is contained in six books of *Carmina.* Even in such stereotyped pieces as *The Seven Liberal Arts,* and *The Seven Capital Sins,* we can glimpse his talent. Besides many minor epistolary pieces to friends, there is the vigorous Christian invective entitled *Paraenesis to His Judges,* a stirring condemnation of the judges who condemned him to prison.

The piece for which he is known, however, *Gloria, laus et honor* (*Opera* 69) comprises only the first twenty-two lines of a much longer poem on Palm Sunday and it has been incorporated into the Roman liturgical celebration of this feast. It begins with the poet's shout of praise to the Messiah as he rides along the road to Jerusalem,

Gloria, laus et honor tibi sit, Rex Christe, Redemptor,

[35] On Theodulf, see Raby, *A History of Christian-Latin Poetry,* pp. 171 *ff.*; *cf.* Remy de Gourmont, *Le latin mystique,* pp. 107 *ff.*

echoing the jubilant cries of the children and people as they rush to strew palm branches and garments in the path of the humble Messiah, as He makes his way to the city gates. One of the best known versions of the hymn is from the hand of J. Mason Neale:

All glory, laud and honor
To Thee, Redeemer King,
To Whom the lips of children
Made sweet hosannas ring.
Thou art the King of Israel,
Thou David's royal Son,
Who in the Lord's name comest,
The King and blessed one.
The people of the Hebrews
With palms befort Thee went;
Our praise and prayer and anthems,
Before Thee we present.
To Thee Before Thy Passion
They sang their hymns of praise;
To Thee now high exalted
Our melody we raise.

As in all great Christian poetry, present, past, and future time are resolved into the liturgical present: the commemoration of Palm Sunday. For in the hymn we join our voices with the boys who strewed palms in the Messiah's path, but singing now to a King who reigns in Heaven. Indeed, says the poet, we are naughty boys who have strayed from the virtuous path of our fathers. The hymn ends with the poet's poignant wish that he might at least be the humble donkey that bore the Lord and thus be able to enter with Him into the Holy City. It is a finely conceived poetic vision.

One small group of monastic poets and scholars marked the decline of the Carolingian age: the abbot Rhaban Maurus, and his pupils Walafrid Strabo and Gottschalk.[36] All three were German, all connected with the monasteries of Fulda and Reichenau at one time or another. Rhaban was more the administrator and

[36] See Raby, *A History of Christian-Latin Poetry*, pp. 183 *ff*.; *A History of Secular Latin Poetry*, I.221 *ff*.

stern churchman; Gottschalk, the deepest and perhaps the most unbalanced; Walafrid, a very learned monk with the prudence and good sense to match his poetic ability. Walafrid (about 809–849) studied at Fulda, and was familiarly received by Emperor Louis and his wife Judith whom he calls a second Miriam, "lover of peace, and sweetheart of light." He acted as tutor to the future emperor Charles the Bald, and before his death became abbot of Reichenau. It is hard to believe that he was scarcely eighteen when he translated into hexameters a prose version of *The Visions of Wettin.* Wettin had been his teacher at Reichenau, and in his dying delirium, Wettin, like some primitive Swedenborg, had had visions of hell, purgatory, and heaven, which were taken down in prose. From the beginning, Walafrid showed signs of great poetic virtuosity, and for all its youthfulness, *The Visions of Wettin* are a brilliant foreshadowing of Dante's *Divina commedia.* Like many of his other pieces, he piously dedicated the poem to Grimaldi, the stern abbot of St. Gall, at whose instigation much of Walafrid's work was composed.

The Visions of Wettin show a striking imaginative power: there is a vivid portrait of the damned suffering in Hell for sins of fornication and sodomy; even Charlemagne is bound in Purgatory to atone for his sensuality before he can be admitted to Paradise. Walafrid's personal charm made him the favorite poet at the court of Louis the Pious and his lovely queen; and, when he left, it was through Louis' intervention that he was elevated to the chair of abbot of Reichenau. There, in his leisure hours, Walafrid relaxed by working in a tiny monastic garden on the abbey grounds. It was a real garden plot, filled with all the useful and precious herbs that we read of from the middle ages; but it was the source of inspiration for his happiest poetic creation, *Hortulus,* or *The Care of Gardens.* The description and the care of a garden plot is a commonplace in ancient poetry; but for Walafrid the catalogue of his twenty-two herbs and flowers is not enough. Indeed, the final apostrophe to the Queen of the Garden, the Church, as symbolized in the roses of martyrdom and the lilies of purity and peace, suggests that the entire poem is a delicate allegory of the life of the soul, and of the manifold virtues of the Church on earth, that

Chaste Maid, Spouse of the Bridegroom,
Dove, Bride, Queen, Beloved!

Many of Walafrid's flowers and spices are mentioned in the imperial capitulary, *On Country Houses,* published during the reign of Charlemagne, and Gregory of Tours describes many a monastery garden in his *History of the Franks.* But surely no monastery garden was like this one. The poem begins with the monk's work on the plot to prepare the soil for the tender plants. Then the work of planting, watering, and waiting. Drought and dryness falls; and the monk must fill jars with water and delicately water the growing shoots with his hands. All the herbs of the mediaeval garden are there: fennel, chervil, parsley, sage, rue, wormwood, horehound, and many more. There is a fine sensuousness, an almost Keatsian delight in nature's simple loveliness. But it is when he comes to his roses and lilies that the deeper meaning of the poem begins to emerge. For the roses are the blood of martyrs, the lilies the purity and faith of the Church's virgins and confessors; and she, the inviolate maid, is the fertile source of all this prolific life. All the flowers spring from the root of Jesse, and the red and white are the two aspects of the Church on earth and in heaven, militant and triumphant. The *Hortulus* is far from being a Latin exercise; it almost suggests the pagan vitality of a Catullus immured in a Christian monastery.

Walafrid's comrade Gottschalk (810–869) left Fulda after a disagreement with the domineering Rhaban and sought a dispensation from his vows. A talented, sensitive, and perhaps disturbed young monk, he was all but imprisoned by Maurus in the monastery at Orbais in the diocese of Soissons, in France. Here he began studying theology as well as composing poetry. Unstable, he obtained his ordination at the hands of a bishop of Rheims, then fled from his monastery, and became an itinerant preacher throughout Italy, Dalmatia, and Pannonia. Sermons and treatises poured from his pen, and when he began to teach a kind of twofold predestination, by which God consigned some men to Hell and others to Heaven independent of their merits, he was charged with heresy, condemned by the Council of Quiersy convoked by Hincmar of Rheims, imprisoned and beaten in the convent of Hautvillers. His last years in prison were passed in illness and despair; and he died without the Church's blessing in 869 because of his final refusal to accept the Confession of Faith sent to his bedside by that imperious prelate, Hincmar, Archbishop of Rheims. So died to the world a major poetic talent of the ninth century. Of Gottschalk's work there are extant, besides the theological sermons and treatises, some delicate poetic prayers in novel rhythms and bits of personal poetry. His *Confessions of Faith* are also extant, undoubtedly recited under duress, but of interest nonetheless. There is a beautifully written poetic epistle to his comrade, Ratramnus of Corbie, which closes with a mystical apocalyptic vision:

> They shall never die, whom the Father has given
> To the Son with love, washed in the wave of His Blood.
> For they are the heavenly Lamb's: He gave them life,
> Nor can the Beast, the Brigand, the Lion, Wolf, Dragon,
> Seize them by force or fraud. All those
> Whom He bequeathed to the Father must come to Him.

It is a vision of the sealed testament of the Lamb, the pledge that those who are sealed with his Blood cannot be lost. Its personal implication for Gottschalk himself makes it all the more moving.

But surely his best piece is a poem to an unnamed young man, perhaps a fellow-monk, who had asked Gottschalk to write a *dulce carmen*, "some sweet song." The answer to the request was the well-known *Ut quid iubes, pusiole* (*Opera*, 5), "Little one, you bid me sing," one of the most touching lyrics of the period, full of the torment and sorrow of troubled youth. It begins very calmly,

> Little one, you bid me sing,
> Sing some sweet and tuneful thing
> And this although they've exiled me
> Far out upon a distant sea.
> Why bid me sing?
>
> Tears are simpler, my little lad;
> Gay songs are cruel when one's sad.
> The songs you beg I cannot bear
> Though you ask, I know, from childhood's care,
> My little lad.

He has been in exile on this sea too long; and he thinks of the Jews in Babylonian captivity singing Psalm 136 by the waterways and willows of Babylon. For the early Fathers, like Methodius, the willows were the symbols of temperance and chastity, the rivers were the seas of the world dashing against the senses; and to sing a song to the Lord meant keeping the law in the face of the world's seductions. This too, I think, is at the basis of Gottschalk's quiet imagery. The only song he can find to sing is a doxology to the Godhead reigning in heaven; this will be a sweet song, sung "with my little one" day and night. For the friendship of God and of the little brother who is faithful to him in his misery will give him the heart, at last, to sing. The tragic texture of Gottschalk's life is subtly caught up in his poignant poetry. And though he died without the external viaticum of the Church he loved, we may in any case believe that the last stanzas of the *Ut quid iubes* were somewhere in his heart; it is, in itself, an act of faith and submission to Christ and His revelation:

> But I must needs fulfill your plea,
> For all the hours you spent with me.
> To sing the Father, Son, I am not loath,
> And Him Who doth proceed from both–
> This sing I willingly.
>
> "Blessed art Thou, Almighty One,
> Father, Holy Spirit, Son,
> God united, Three above,
> God of might, justice, love–"
> Gladly, little one.

The doxology closes with a final thought for the "little one" who inspired his song: it is as though in human love Gottschalk saw reflected all his faith and belief. It was his one, tenuous link with the God of might, justice, and love.

Of Rhaban Maurus (780–856), the *praeceptor Germaniae* and abbot of Fulda until his resignation in 842, teacher of Walafrid and Gottschalk, little can be said. A friend of Alcuin (who nicknamed him Maurus, in honor of Benedict's disciple) and, at the end of his life, Archbishop of Mainz, he everywhere displays the intelligence and industry of a well-educated German monk, without enjoying any really creative talent. All we can say of his elegies, hymns, and poetic epistles is that they display a certain facility. It is at best an uncertain tradition that assigns to him the well-known *Veni, Creator Spiritus,* the solemn acclamation sung on the occasion of the crowning of kings and pontiffs and at the translation of holy relics. Part of the hymn's elusive charm is its compactness: in six short strophes all the theology of the Holy Spirit is expressed. Used at Rheims in the middle of the eleventh century, none of the manuscripts go back beyond the tenth. It consists mostly in a series of invocations: the Spirit is Source, Fire, Anointing, strength against the enemies of the Church, the cause of peace and harmony. Even if Maurus did not write it, it must surely come from the environment of the Carolingian revival.

Good Trinitarian hymnody is rare in the early Church; there are fragments of poetic inspiration in the doxologies of Ambrose and Hilary. Perhaps the finest doxologies are really those to be found in the poems of Gottschalk, in his "Little one, you bid me sing," and at the close of his epistle to Ratramnus of Corbie quoted above. In the seventh century there are attributed to the Greek Father Maximus the Confessor three long supplications in verse to the Godhead; they reflect his own calm acceptance of the Christian mystery, and the omnipotent providence of God; but, though well constructed and carefully metrical, they are hardly inspired work at best.

Quite a different atmosphere is reflected in the twelfth century poem, *Veni Sancte Spiritus,* "Come, Holy Ghost," which was incorporated into the Pentecost liturgy:

> Veni, sancte Spiritus,
> Et emitte caelitus
> Lucis tuae radium.

According to the best evidence, there is little reason to doubt that it was composed by Stephen Langton, the talented Archbishop of Canterbury (*d.* 1228), rather than, as some would believe, Pope Innocent III (*d.* 1216). In any case, it is the finest Pentecostal hymn in the literature of the Church. The Golden Sequence, as it has aptly been called, has the regular structure of a typical Roman liturgical prayer: in the opening stanzas there is an apostrophe to the Spirit implying all the divine powers He possesses as a source of man's good; the second part contains the urgent petition. The charm of the poem lies in the sharply etched antitheses: the Spirit is a Ray of comfort, a brilliant Light, a welcome guest; He brings coolness in time of heat, rest in toil, comfort amid tears. The last lines are most beautiful: man is dirty, parched, wounded, stiff, twisted, and cold—he is, in short, like a dead body left full of wounds on some forgotten mediaeval battlefield. Only the Spirit can fill him with life and moisture, heat and the health of moral goodness. The dry, cold theology of the schoolroom melts under the poetic image:

Lava, quod est sordidum,
riga, quod est aridum,
sana, quod est saucium.

No version can do it justice:

Wash the soiled body,
Moisten what is dry,
Heal all that is wounded,
Bend all that is rigid,
Fire what is cold,
Straighten what is crooked.

Mary: Woman and Virgin

CHAPTER NINE

HIPPOLYTUS of Rome (*d.* 235) wrote one of the earliest commentaries on the *Song of Songs*, and even though we can study the complete text only in a Georgian version, it is clear that Ambrose made good use of it for his series of treatises on virginity. Origen's homilies and commentary on the Canticle followed some years later. Both Hippolytus and Origen identified the Bride of the Canticle with the Church and the soul; Ambrose seems to have been the first to apply the imagery to the Virgin, though even in doing this he seems to have been influenced by Hippolytus' language. The full, allegorical interpretation emerges finally in the sermons of Bernard: here the maiden of the Song is the Church, the Christian soul, the Virgin, the monk, and, finally, the privileged soul of the mystic.

Here, in the collection of love-songs gathered together under the title, the *Song of Songs,* we have a rich source of imagery for the growing literature and poetry dedicated to the Virgin Mary. In addition, there was the identification as the Second Eve, crushing the Serpent's head, and this was connected by some (who are already quoted by Methodius about A.D. 290), with the Woman of the Apocalypse who escapes the Dragon and brings forth her child in the wilderness. She is spoken of as the Wisdom of the Old Testament sapiential books: the *Hokmah* that played before the Deity before the earth was made, and whose delight was to be with the children of men. All the noble women of the

Old Law, Ruth, Judith, Esther, Miriam, and the rest—all contribute to the Marian symbolism. Thus developed an exotic landscape of Oriental flower-gardens, and sensuous love-imagery, which served as the background for the battle of the courageous woman against the powers of darkness for the life of her child, the Christian soul. Indeed, throughout there is the subtle parallelism suggested between Mary as Christ's Mother and the Church the Virgin Mother of all the baptized. Still other images clustered about the New Testament mysteries: the nine months of expectancy, the Flight before Herod, the encounter at the foot of the Cross, and all the other Gospel events in which Mary was closely involved. These formed the content of many *kontakia* and hymns of the Eastern Church, especially those of Ephraem the Syrian, Romanos Melodos, John Damascene, and later Byzantine singers like John Mauropus and Ignatius the Deacon.

Perhaps the greatest poet of the early Church is St. Ephraem of Nisibis (*d.* 373), whose father was a pagan Syrian priest. It was Ephraem who popularized the forms of Syriac poetry in the Eastern Church, especially the so-called *memrâ*, the *madrâshâ*, and the *sogithâ*. The *memrâ* was not so much a hymn but a poetic homily, with lines of counted syllables. The *madrâshâ* and the *sogitha*, on the other hand, were sung: the former composed in set strophes with a recurring refrain to be sung by the people; the *sogithâ* was divided into strophes to be sung by two choirs or precentors and thus lent itself to dramatic poems. Both of these hymn-forms, as well as the metrical homily, had a strong influence on the Byzantine Greek *kontakion*. St. Ephraem composed many Syriac hymns and metrical homilies of great length and complexity. For the Syriac Christians they formed a magnificent poetic corpus of doctrinal instruction, biblical commentary, and refutation of the current heresies.

Ephraem's poetic imagery has the brightness and vividness of the Orient: he likes symbols of light and heat, the flash of precious gems, the smell of exotic perfumes, and images drawn from clouds and ship-sailing, from the harvest of wheat, wine and oil. It is to Christ and His Mother that Ephraem pays the highest tribute of his poetic genius. Throughout he adapts the images of the Old and New Testaments: Christ is the Lion, the Light of man, the Gate, the Oil in the lamps, the Pearl of great price, the leaven in the great lump of humanity. In the great thirty-first *Hymn on the Church and Virginity* (ed. T. J. Lamy), he speaks of Jesus as the cluster of grapes, the germ of wheat, the mirror held up to man, man's medicine, the intrepid sailor bringing His ship to port, the furnace of the world which tests the gold and silver of our actions. Indeed, fire and light imagery is the favorite of Ephraem. Christ is not only a furnace, he is a burning coal (*Hymn on the Church* 17)—the symbol of purity and strength, and of awesome decision. Mary is like a bright cloud embracing the Sun (*Hymn on Our Lady* 19); at Jesus' conception, the Logos entered Mary's womb by way of her ear (*Hymn on Our Lady* 11). It was at that moment that the Virgin chastely enclosed the Son like a hot coal (*Hymn on Our Lady* 19); for He was the Fire in her virgin body: Christ the giant of the ages confined within a narrow womb, God in the world (*ibid.* 10).

It is interesting to note that Ephraem's Syriac hymns in Greek translation had an important influence on the work of the sixth century Romanos, so-called Melodos, a converted Syriac Jew who became a deacon at Constantinople. Though not as great or original a poet as Ephraem, Romanos is far superior to Gregory of Nazianzus and brought the Byzantine hymn-form to its ultimate poetic development. Romanos reflects none of the classical form, none of the pagan reminiscences of Gregory; his hymns breathe the incense of the Greek Liturgy, and their dramatic fire echoes the austere message of the primitive Gospel. His *kontakia* are delicately patterned stanzas after the model of the *madrâshâ*, their initial letters giving an acrostic identification: "This song is by the humble Romanos." Of those which seem certainly from his pen—not all of the eighty-five attributed to him have been completely edited—the best known are a *Christmas Hymn*, an *Easter Hymn*, *St. Joseph*, and *Judas Iscariot*.

Most charming of all are the passages in which Romanos sings of the Virgin. For him she is the mystical ladder by which (inverting the Platonic imagery) the Word, the divine Physician, descended to bring medicine and healing to men. The Christmas Cave is the place of mystery wherein the inaccessible Light revealed Himself to creatures. All the details of Jesus' life are, in

Romanos, invested in a mystic, sacramental aura: to dramatize them is to bring grace and sweetness to mortals. He conveys a sense of Christian gnosis; for the ineffable secret of Jesus' birth "Thou hast told to no one," he tells us in the *Akathistos* hymn (if it is from his pen), and yet it has been revealed to a young virgin alone. Romanos is the clearest and sweetest of the Byzantine singers, surely the finest Christian poetry in Greek. His genius captured and enshrined the primitive Church's atmosphere of ritual mystery, transforming it into the stuff of liturgical song. His imagery is sparse, but his dramatic verse breathes a simple grace that is impossible to recapture in any version.

The Marian hymn of the Latin West was much more austere and rhetorical than that of the East. The Latin hymn is usually concise, centers on a single mystery or event, and absolves the praise of the Virgin in a series of antitheses (Eve-Mary, virgin-mother, creature bearing creator) or simple acclamations (door, star, gate, guide, mother, etc.). There is a quite charming early hymn, *Quem terra, pontus, aethera,* attributed by some to Venantius Fortunatus, and though not surely from his hand it certainly belongs to the pre-Caroline era.

> Him Whom earth, air, sea adore,
> Worship and proclaim as threefold governance
> Of the world, Mary bears within her cell.

"Cell," here, *claustrum,* can mean "prison," "fortress," even "cloister." The confining of the world's creator in a narrow womb is the poem's central antithesis; that the Lord of all living things had to drink milk from a virgin's breast. Again Eve is mentioned and the reversal of roles; the poet ends with an appeal to all redeemed mankind to "applaud the virgin who restored our life"; she is the gate of the High King, the dazzling door of Light.

The high point of Marian hymnody is reached in the ninth, tenth, and eleventh centuries, especially through the influence of Benedictine monachism throughout the European continent. Of the great number extant, three will concern us here: *Ave Maris Stella,* perhaps from about the eighth or ninth century; *Alma Redemptoris Mater,* from the twelfth; and the prose rhythm *Salve Regina,* attributed to Herman the Cripple.

The *Ave Maris Stella, Hail, Star of the Sea,* occurs as early as the ninth century in a manuscript of St. Gall, and is really a hymn on the feast of the Annunciation. The poet takes up the greeting *Ave* from the Angel of the Gospel story: she is an *alma mater,* a source of nourishment for her children; she is the Star of the Sea, the sailors' star to guide her sons on life's voyage. (In the thirteenth century collection of John Garland, entitled *Stella Maris,*[37] there is an entire poem devoted to Mary as the Pole Star presiding over the other constellations of the Zodiac.) Our anonymous poet goes on in the second stanza to tell of Mary's reception of the angel's *Ave:* she inverted it to *Eva,* magically signifying her role in the process of salvation,

> *funda nos in pace*
> *mutans nomen Evae,*
> "changing Eva's name,"

but also, if we follow the Latin, changing the name *e vae,* "from woe." The rest of the hymn is a petition: we are blind and in chains, the results of our sin; Mary can release us, and finally prepare our journey to God. Mary's preternatural powers are thus suggested by the miraculous greeting of the angel together with her inversion of the *Ave.*

The *Alma Redemptoris Mater,* which follows closely within the same poetic tradition, seems to reflect the Benedictine tradition.[38] It had been attributed to Hermann the Cripple (Contractus), a monk of Reichenau who died in 1054; but the oldest manuscripts seem not to go back farther than the thirteenth century. With its six quantitative hexameter lines the hymn seems an anachronism; it is to some extent a metrical paraphrase of the earlier one. The poet sees the Virgin as the North Star, and the ever-open gate of

[37] See Raby, *A History of Christian-Latin Poetry,* pp. 385 *ff.*; and for the text, see the edition of Evelyn F. Wilson (Cambridge, Mass., 1946), n. 6., with the commentary.

[38] See my article, "The Mediaeval Hymn, *Alma Redemptoris:* A Linguistic Analysis," *Classical Journal* 52 (1957), 171–74, with the bibliography. For good treatments of Marian symbolism, see Hugo Rahner, *Maria und die Kirche* (Innsbruck, 1951), and A. Müller, *Ecclesia-Maria* (Freiburg, 1951).

heaven, and begs her to save the people who are falling or sinking (*cadenti . . . populo*). Finally, in virtue of her miraculous bearing of her creator, symbolized in the *Ave*, he prays for mercy on all sinners. The hymn has a charming ambiguity: the falling and rising of the people may be from sin, or the reference could be to rising and falling stars, or even to stumbling children. The traditional title of Star of the Sea seems again to refer to the pole star, by which sailors might steer their ships at night. And even the gate of heaven may have a zodiacal connotation: Macrobius uses the expression "gate of the sun" to refer to the constellations Cancer and Aries—the two constellations in which the solstice occurs, when the sun seems, as it were, to pause in its path around the ecliptic.

The hymn is not personal but communal; it is a monastic prayer for the sinful community of men, beginning with a eulogy and ending with a petition. The Mother of the Redeemer is pictured as the fixed pole-star guiding men across the sea of life; again, she is a celestial passageway ever passable and accessible. Loving mankind, she is asked to come to the aid of those who are ever falling and striving to rise again. But the falling here has overtones of stars fading from their place in heaven, of children needing a mother's help in walking, perhaps even of sinking ships striving to stay afloat. The final petition closes with an abridged reference to the miraculous message of the angel, the *Ave* that changed to *Eva*. Despite the calm of the last few lines, it is an extremely devotional poem; and its force derives from the subtle imagery of the first few lines: Mary, the fixed pole to guide sinking, stumbling men. With good reason was it beloved in the days of Chaucer, who seems to refer to it in his *Prioresses Tale:*

> This litel childe, his litel book lerninge,
> As he sat in the scole at his prymer
> He *Alma Redemptoris* herde singe,
> As children lerned hir antiphoner;
> And, as he dorste, he drough him ner and ner,
> And herkned ay the wordes and the note,
> Til he the firste vers coude al by rote.

Another lovely prose-hymn attributed to Hermann of Reichenau is the *Hail, Holy Queen.* But according to one reliable theory, it goes back to a contemporary of Hermann: Aimar, bishop of Le Puy, in France, some time in the eleventh century. Once again, at the opening of the *Salve Regina,* we have an echo of the angelic message, "Hail," together with a series of acclamations; but here the special reason for the petition is the general exile of Eve's children from the garden of Paradise. The sweet Virgin is asked to turn her eyes from heaven to look upon those who dwell in the tearful valleys of earth. She herself will mark the end of man's exile by granting them a vision of the Son she bore.

Even to list the various Marian symbols would require many pages. It was, however, the poetry of the mediaeval Franciscan movement that refired the cold rhetoric of earlier centuries to create a devotional hymnody that was truly of the people. A particularly favored topic was the so-called Compassion of the Virgin, Mary's own share in the sufferings of Christ's Passion and Death. Here too, there was the influence of Byzantine and Romanesque paintings or illuminations of Pieta-groups or of the Sorrowful Virgin at the foot of the gibbet. Such indeed was the imaginative background of the *Stabat Mater,* a liturgical sequence that is one of the most ecstatic products of Franciscan spirituality. Three manuscripts of the late fourteenth or early fifteenth centuries attribute it to the Franciscan friar, Jacopone da Todi, who died in 1306 after a life of exciting adventure.[39] Jacopone did compose a poetic *lauda* entitled *La Donna del Paradiso*, a dramatic vision of Mary and the apostle John at the foot of the Cross. But most modern scholars would tend to discredit the manuscript evidence which would make him the author of the *Stabat Mater*. The *Donna del Paradiso* has a fast-moving dramatic pace which follows the Virgin from the trial of Jesus right until his broken body is taken from the Cross and laid in her arms. Despite its highly charged emotional tone it possesses a tenderness and an austere charm that recall the dramatic kontakia of the Greek

[39] On Jacopone da Todi (*c.* 1230–1306), see the brief article and bibliography in F. L. Cross, *The Oxford Dictionary of the Christian Church*, p. 710. *Cf.* also Raby, *A History of Christian-Latin Poetry*, pp. 436 *ff*., and Remy de Gourmont, *Le latin mystique* (Paris, 1930), pp. 375 *ff*.

Romanos. At the first sight of her Son stumbling along the Via Dolorosa, the Virgin cries out to Him in a mother's lament:

> *O figlio, figlio, figlio, figlio, amoroso giglio—*

it is almost a ritual incantation:

> My Son, my Son, my Son, my Son, my lovely lily!
> Dear eyes of my Son, can you not answer me?
> Why do you hide from the breasts that suckled you?

And later, from the Cross, Jesus in agony consoles her:

> *Mamma, perchè ti lagni?*
> Mamma, why do you so lament? . . .
> Look, I entrust you to the arms of John,
> John, my chosen one, to be your son.

Finally, as she kisses His lifeless body, she sings a lament that reaches to all the mothers of the world:

> My Son, white and red, beyond compare,
> My Son, white and fair,
> Son of once joyful countenance—
> Why has the world despised you?

As we compare this with the Latin poem, we are quite struck with the contrast. The *Stabat Mater,* for all its emotional atmosphere, has a completely different tonality and approach.[40] In comparison with the Italian poem its structure is quite taut, with a complex rhythmic and rhyme scheme. Quite different from the dramatic structure of the *lauda,* the Latin poem is composed in the prayer-form: the first part (stanzas (1–4) is a narrative of Mary's compassion: "she stood . . . He hung . . . the sword pierced." Then, in the second (5–10), is the petition. It is a personal meditation before a picture or statuary group of the Crucifixion; and the votary asks to feel the pain of Mary's Compassion, even to suffer the wounds of the Cross, to be associated in the sorrow, to be drunk with the blood. The final appeal is that the Virgin may protect the poet on the Judgment Day, and

[40] See the bibliography under "Stabat Mater," in Cross, *Oxford Dictionary of the Christian Church,* p. 1285.

lead him to Paradise (9-10). The pious votary asks to feel the pain and the misery of the Virgin, and in this way to achieve penitence and the grace of final perseverance. The poem was chanted by the masochistic Flagellants of the fourteenth century, and it is in its way a great religious document; but it lacks focus and unity, and seems excessive in its vast orgy of emotion. Though long in use in Germany, France, and England, and a source of inspiration to many great musical composers, it was not admitted to the Roman Missal until the eighteenth century.

Such were the fortunes of Marian hymnody down to the Middle Ages. Bernard of Cluny,[41] who was born at Morlas in the Pyrenees and flourished in the middle of the twelfth century, is best known for his bitter satire, *On Contempt of the World,* which he dedicated to his abbot, Peter the Venerable. It is a denunciation of the sins of both laity and clergy that goes beyond anything Juvenal ever wrote. In fact he says that if the great satirists of old, Horace, Lucilius, Persius, and Juvenal, would come back to earth, even they would be shocked, and they would realize that theirs was a Golden Age in comparison. It is a long, disturbing poem, written in acid; and Bernard's fanatic voice sounds a dread note of warning for sinners. The only relief comes in the vision of the *Urbs Syon aurea,* "Golden city of Sion, milk-white home, famed for those who dwell therein." It is an almost ecstatic cry of hope as the pilgrim glimpses his goal:

> City unique, mystic mansion built in heaven,
> My joy is for thee, my sorrow for myself,
> Breathless in my sorrow. Often in spirit
> I visit thee, for in the body I cannot.
> Flesh is earth, and earth is flesh; no longer
> Can I stand. . . .

We are all perhaps familiar with this poem from the beautiful translation introduced into English hymnals by J. M. Neale. There is also the rhythmic version of the poet Swinburne which begins,

[41] On Bernard of Cluny, see Max Manitius, *Geschichte der lateinischen Literatur des Mittelalters,* III. 780 *ff.;* Curtius, *op. cit.,* p. 122; Cross, *op. cit.,* p. 161.

O land without guilt, strong city, safe built in a marvelous place,
I cling to thee, ache for thee, sing to thee, wake for thee,
 watch for thy face:
Full of cursing and strife are the days of my life, with their
 sins they are fed,
Out of sin is the root, unto sin is the fruit, in their
 sins they are dead.

And it continues farther on:

Yet through faith I require thee, through hope I desire thee, in
 hope I hold fast,
Crying out, day and night, that my soul may have sight of thy
 joy at the last.

It is the heavenly Jerusalem of the Apocalypse that is the constant object of his search; as yet, he can only enter it in imagination and spirit. Despite the monk's mortal weakness, he walks the path with the strength of Jesus as he makes for his true home. There he will find food and drink, love and peace of soul beyond all tragedy or tears. But the golden passage on the city of Sion is only an interlude, and the poem soon reverts to his tone of whining and recrimination, and thus the poem soon becomes tiresome and unreal.

The same Bernard of Cluny, however, was very probably the author of a charming collection of Marian pieces called the *Mariale* (a word formed like the Latin *Missale*), or Mary-book. It consists of fifteen poems in praise of the Virgin, beginning with a paraphrase of the Psalm:

Like the hot stag at the stream,
So the soul of the Christian
Hastens to the fountain
Of living water, God.

This is the poem which contains the well-known lines,

Daily, daily,
Sing to Mary,

and continues to develop the theological allegorism with which we have been familiar. It is Mary, again, who represents the divine quality of mercy, interceding for the sinner against the austere justice of the eternal Father. It is a role that the Virgin often plays in mediaeval poetry. She becomes the *patrona* before the divine tribunal, an antidote against the despair that theological severity could lead to. Such a charming portrait of the Virgin in Bernard of Cluny is a welcome note in the poetry of the man who wrote in *On Contempt of the World,*

> Women are beasts; their sins are like the sands.

Apart from the Virgin, women are totally corrupt and sensuous, in Bernard's eyes, as untrustworthy as vipers, a "sweet poison," "lovely corruption." A fellow monk, Odo of Cluny, continues the same misogynist tradition by borrowing a theme we have seen earlier in St. John Chrysostom; in his *Conferences* (book 2) he wrote:

> The beauty of a woman is only skin-deep. If men could only see what is beneath the flesh and penetrate below the surface with eyes like the Boeotian lynx, they would be nauseated just to look at women. For all this feminine charm is nothing but phlegm, blood, humors, gall. Just imagine all that is hidden in nostrils, throat, and stomach. ...We are repelled to touch vomit or ordure even with our fingertips. How then can we ever want to embrace what is merely a sack of rottenness?

Even Chrysostom hardly went as far as the masters of Cluny. Juvenal's Sixth Satire is tame and austere by comparison. Today, the excessive virulence seems almost incomprehensible.

Of the great poetic talent of Peter Abelard (1079–1142) we shall have to speak in detail farther on. The famous hymn for the Annunciation which is attributed to him is almost certainly not from his hand. It begins with:

> To the Virgin He sent not any angel
> But his own archangel, Courage, lover
> Of Men. For it was a brave messenger
> We needed, as witness to nature's shock
> At the birth of His Son from a virgin.

But it soon falls into the usual rhetorical antitheses which made the fortunes of so many Marian hymns. Gone is the fire of

Paulinus and Venantius Fortunatus, or the monastic sincerity of the *Alma Redemptoris Mater*. It is a pity that Thomas Aquinas or his Dominican circle did not produce a Sequence on the Virgin Mary, or a hymn that could rival in theological accuracy the poems of the Office of the Blessed Sacrament.

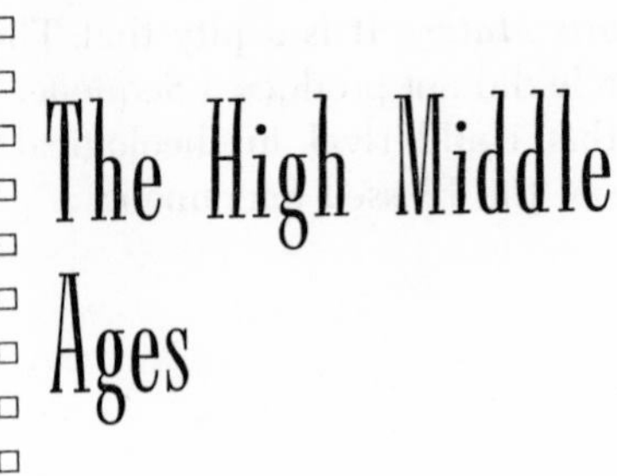

The High Middle Ages

CHAPTER TEN

BY THE eleventh, twelfth, and thirteenth centuries, secular and religious poetry had developed into a vast variety of types. Much of our evidence must be drawn from a number of anonymous collections, as for example the Cambridge Songs, the *Carmina Burana* of Benediktbeuern, the Arundel Collection, and the songs of the Vatican manuscript (Vat. Lat. 4389).[42] The Cambridge Songs would appear to be a German song-book, the bulk of the pieces coming from the eleventh century. There is the famous lyric tale about Heriger, Bishop of Mainz, who confuted a self-styled prophet that had claimed to have visited heaven and hell; another, in sequence form, about a snow-child, and how the husband punished his wayward wife. One of the most charming of the collection is *Levis exsurgit Zephyrus,* the lament of a nun alone in her cell in the springtime: as all life seems to blossom outside, she alone seems to represent pallor, languor, death—*nam mea languet anima,* "for my soul is faint. . . ." It would appear that all or most of these lyrics were meant to be sung, and they were perhaps performed by wandering minstrels at feasts or public gatherings.

The most famous of all mediaeval collections comes from a

[42] See Manitius, *op. cit.,* pp. 966 *ff.;* and see the edition by A. Hilka and O. Schumann, *Carmina Burana* (3 vols. in 2, Heidelberg, 1930, 1930 and 1941), with commentary. In my references, however, I have retained the older, and better known, numbering of Schmeller.

manuscript preserved for many years in the Benedictine monastery of Benediktbeuern in Bavaria. Acquired by the Royal Library at Munich (as Monacensis Lat. 4660) it was first edited by the librarian Andreas Schmeller in 1847 under the title of *Carmina Burana,* "Songs from Benediktbeuern," the title it has claimed ever since. This curious collection was perhaps made by a monk of the monastery in the fourteenth century; some of the earliest and the best songs come from the twelfth century; the latest reflect the influence of German minnesingers of the late thirteenth. They are proof, if any were needed, of the incredible richness of the age. There are some charming boy-girl lyrics and pastourelles: there is the lovely Latin-German poem on the girl with the red dress that rustles (*Carmina Burana-CB* 138), the shepherdess and the scholar (*CB* 63), the lament of the maid forsaken (*CB* 58), poems to the springtime such as "Hail, Longed for Spring" (*CB* 156), or on scholars giving up their books (*CB* 48). Exceptionally well conceived is the lyric on sleep, *Dum Dianae vitrea* (*CB* 37): it is a pagan poem on the joys of sleep as the moon rises and the water churns over the millstones; and the sensuous sounds with the smell of fresh grass make it quite unique in mediaeval poetry, and reminds us rather of Sappho's poem on the precinct of Venus—or Shelley as he might have written in the thirteenth century:[43]

> 'Tis late, and Diana lights her crystal lamp
> From her brother Apollo's rosy glow. The sweet
> Zephyr's breath blows away the clouds.
> Hearts are soothed with lyre strings
> And moved once more to love. And to all men
> The evening star's gay light grants the grateful
> Dew of sleep—sleep, a happy medicine of man,
> Calming the storms of pain and care, slipping
> Into the closed eyelids, whose coming is like the joy
> Of love. Through the weary brain Sleep draws a soft
> Wind that blows over ripe grain, with the murmur
> Of streams flowing on pure sand, and the whining
> Of millstones round and round, stealing the light

[43] *Cf.* also Helen Waddell, *Medieval Latin Lyrics* (London, 1957), pp. 264 *ff.* with the note.

From eyes full of drowsy sleep....
The nightingale mourns under the lovely arbor.
It is sweet so to sleep....

For this is the theme of the poem: sleep and love become a symbol of man's final happiness; they are the focal point of all the loveliness of the world.

In the same collection (*CB* 92) there is a peculiarly surrealist piece on a roast swan, *Once I Dwelt by Waters Fair* (*Olim lacus colueram*), which recalls the whimsical and sometimes macabre paintings of Hieronymus Bosch and must surely be a product of Germany or the Lowlands. Implicit in it is the old pagan proverb, that swans sing most sweetly only before their death; but our swan is already dead, merrily roasting over a kitchen hearth. The song is put into the mouth of the swan itself: plaintively it recalls the free life it led on distant waters, now that it is being spitted and basted for a monastic banquet. *Miser, miser,* "Alas, alack," is the repeated refrain:

Once I dwelt by waters fair,
Once handsome, without care,
Once a lovely swan was I.
    Alas, alack!
    Burnt black am I,
    And roasted thoroughly.
Once I was as white as snow;
And now, blacker than a crow—
I the loveliest of birds.
    Alas, alack! etc.
How hot the pyre burns!
As the cook just turns and turns
And the servant takes a taste.
    Alas, alack! etc.
Would I were on waters fair
Even under the naked air—
Not smothered in this sauce.
    Alas, alack! etc.
Now in a serving dish I lie;
All too late—I cannot fly!
Just see their flashing teeth—.
    Alas, alack!

Burnt black am I,
And roasted thoroughly.

The final stanza shows the miserable swan carried from the spit to the banquet table, ready to be torn by the hungry, flashing teeth of the guests. As a piece of virtuosity it is quite advanced for its day, and reminds us of the apotheosis song of Horace (*Odes* II.20) in which the poet mockingly pictures himself being transmogrified into a swan. But in our Roast Swan Song I have the impression that there is a bit of whimsical mediaeval allegory lurking in the background. The constant refrain, *Miser, miser,* "Alas, alack," the turning on the spit, and the prodding of the cooks suggest a macabre mock-serious vision of the damned in Hell, with the white swan that "dwelt by waters fair" as a symbol of the once innocent Christian soul. There is another swan-song (*CB* 167), with which it possibly may be compared, *Sic mea fata canendo solor:*

It comforts me to sing about my fate
Like the swan when close to death. My color pales,
And a tender pang invades my heart.
Woe never ceases;
Travail increases;
All my powers fly;
Alas, I die!
Dying, dying, dying—alas!

These descriptions of death are frequent in mediaeval verse. But the poet is not really dying; he is in love. It is the love-death ecstasy (which we have seen, in another context, in Gregory of Nyssa and in Bernard's commentary on the *Song of Songs*) which is the theme of the poem:

I am not loved, though I am doomed to love;
And if she whom I desire would but have pity,
I should be happier than Jove.

Connected in spirit with the *Carmina Burana* are the poems and songs of a number of scholars, clerics, and hangers-on, that some have wrongly grouped together under the misleading title of the Goliards. Three of the most talented of these flourished about the middle of the twelfth century, Hugh Primas of Orleans, the German Archpoet, and Walter of Châtillon.[44] All of these adopt a pseudo-prophetic tone in their castigation of clerical vices, especially Walter of Châtillon with his *Missus sum in vineam:*

> Sent was I to the vineyard:
> The time was three o'clock....

But it may be that the canons and bishops they criticize were precisely the ones who, wearied with the poets' begging and importunities, finally showed them the door. The so-called Archpoet was a follower (parasite is perhaps the better word) of Rainald of Cassel, Archbishop of Cologne, and it was to him that he addressed the classical Goliardic poem, *The Confession:*

> Burning within like a raging fire
> I must express my bitter ire....

But the poem is a roguish caricature of sacramental confession. It is a completely unrepentant admission of guilt for sins of the flesh, wine-bibbing, and general licentiousness. He begs the Archbishop to restore him to favor; and, instead of a firm resolution of amendment he brazenly sings:

> In a tavern I firmly resolve to die
> With tankards of wine standing close by;
> Then will chant the angelic choirs:
> God keep this drunkard from hell's fires.

The *Confession* of the Archpoet is a far cry from St. Augustine; only mediaeval Christianity could tolerate this oddly shaped religious lampoon.

But it is the serious composers of religious hymns who keep close to the stream of traditional symbolism. Perhaps one of the greatest sequences of the early Middle Ages, the *Victimae Paschali,* was written by an obscure Burgundian or Swabian

[44] On Hugh Primas and the Archipoeta, see Manitius, *op. cit.*, pp. 973 *ff.;* and on Walter of Châtillon, pp. 930 *ff.* On the so-called Goliards in general, Helen Waddell's delightful book, *The Wandering Scholars* (London, 1932). See also Raby, *A History of Secular Latin Poetry,* II. 171 *ff.*, for a discussion of Hugh Primas, the Archipoeta, and their circle.

priest named Wipo, who was chaplain to Conrad II and died about the year 1050. Wipo had some knowledge of Sallust, Horace, Vergil, Lucan, Statius, and other writers of the now distant classical past. In his other pieces he liked rhyming Leonine hexameters; but the *Victimae* is composed in a rhythmic prose with occasional isosyllabic correspondence. The poem begins as a vivid vision of Easter morn, as seen by the Christian community celebrating the Paschal liturgy. Thus two levels are juxtaposed: mentally they are swept back in time to meditate on the meaning of the Atonement, summed up in the image of single combat, the fierce duel between Life and Death. Suddenly the poet brings us back to Jerusalem to speak to Mary Magdalen, the first breathless witness of Christ's triumph. It is her we believe, rather than the false rumors of an empty, violated tomb spread by the Jews. But the verses against the *turba Iudaica* were deleted from the version incorporated into the modern Roman missal: those for whom the Saviour died, for whose forgiveness He prayed, should not be scornfully referred to on the morning of His exaltation, now that

Death and Life
Have met in mortal strife.
Though dead, He reigns,
The Lord of Life.
Ah, Mary, can you say
What you saw on the way?

In Mary's gentle heart lies the secret evidence of the mystery; on her testimony we renew our act of faith in the final stanza:

We know that He is risen
Truly from the dead.
O Victor, King!
Have mercy!

The final invocation serves to recall us to the liturgical present with a communal act of faith in the Paschal Victim now reigning gloriously. Past and future, Image and Reality, thus become one in the symbolical liturgical present of the Easter ritual. If the humble priest Wipo had written nothing else he could claim immortality for this simple devotional hymn.

Two great philosopher-poets stand apart from the general movement of monastic piety: Peter Abelard or Abailard (1070–1142)[45] and Alan of Lille (1128–1202). Some of Abelard's most intense pieces are a series of six *Planctus* or laments he composed on scenes from the Old Testament: there is the complaint of Israel for the death of Samson; the mourning of the maidens of Israel for the sacrifice of the daughter of Jephthah; the lament of David at the death of Jonathan. The last *planctus*, the *Lament for Jonathan,* begins:

> So pierced with thee I would that I could lie:
> No greater love could do more than I would.
> To live without thee would be death, slow death,
> Even had I the heart, but half a heart.

And it concludes:

> Peace! I can sing no more. Would my tears
> Could dry up with my song. My hands are bruised
> From beating, hoarse my voice, my soul is faint.

The rhymes are simple enough; but the language itself is quite subtle and complex. The laments, indeed, may well have represented allegorically incidents in Abelard's own life, had we but the clue.

In his hymns, or (using the Hebrew word) *Tillim,* composed for the Missal and divine office, Abelard created a new verse form, which was, however, inspired by the Hebrew psalms and perhaps owed much to Prudentius and Venantius. There is the vitality and the symbolism of Ambrose and of Prudentius' *Cathemerinon:* the dawn suggesting the light of conversion, the revela-

[45] On Peter Abelard in general see the summary article and bibliography in Cross, pp. 3–4; *cf.* also Manitius, *op. cit.,* pp. 195 *ff.,* and Raby, *A History of Secular Latin Poetry,* II.5 *ff.* and 325. There are excellent translations of several of Abelard's lyrics in Waddell, *Mediaeval Latin Lyrics,* pp. 162–69. For a good translation and commentary on the *Historia calamitatum,* see T. Muckle, *The Story of Abelard's Adversities,* with an Introduction by Etienne Gilson (Pontifical Institute of Mediaeval Study., Toronto, 1954); but on the authenticity of the *History* Gilson remained non-committal. For a summary of Abelard's philosophical and theological ideas one may consult Gilson, *History of Christian Philosophy,* pp. 153–63, with the bibliography and notes, pp. 625–30; see also Leff, *Medieval Thought,* pp. 107–114.

tion of Christ and his resurrection. Perhaps the most beautiful is the Vesper hymn for Saturdays beginning *O quanta, qualia sunt illa sabbata/quae semper celebrat superna curia!*

> Ah, what great Sabbaths there shall be
> When we shall celebrate in heaven!
> Rest for the weary, a prize for the brave—
> And God in all for all eternity.

Truly, he says, the heavenly Jerusalem is a city of peace and supreme delight, where desire and achievement are one.

> Ah, the King, the court, the palace;
> What peace, what rest, what joy is there!
> Let those alone who know it speak—
> If even they can find the words.

The vision of the Apocalypse once again draws him on; but now it is more rational and calm, without the hysteria of Bernard of Cluny's *Urbs Syon.* In Abelard there is at once more humanity and a deeper theology.

There is much more to the *corpus* of poetry attributed to Peter Abelard, all of it deserving of serious study. In the face of such great poetic talent, however, one is perhaps embarrassed to read the *Story of My Adversities,* or *Historia calamitatum,* a somewhat hypocritical self-revelation attributed to his pen. We are prepared to accept the naive account of the seduction of the young and beautiful Héloise, the story of the lovers' tortured guilt, the terrible revenge exacted of Abelard and his retaliation—even though the style resembles a romantic mediaeval *novella.* But the arrogant and barefaced tale of Abelard's rise to academic and monastic power, his double-dealing and betrayals, and finally the attempt of his fellow-monks to waylay him on the road, or even by poisoning his Mass wine—all of this is very difficult to credit. It is hard to forge precise links between the events of the *Story* and the life of the theologian Abelard as we know it from more reliable sources; and it may be that this entire narrative of seduction and monastic chicanery is a mediaeval forgery. This is not to deny that it has a precious flavor of its own; and, whether authentic or not, it is essential reading as a revelation of one side at least of the period that produced Bernard's *Sermons on the Song of Songs.*

Another remarkable philosopher-poet of the period was Master Alanus de Insulis, or Alan of Lille as we know him, a speculative thinker of wide reading, who gave up his chair at the University of Paris to spend the last years of his life in the Abbey of Citeaux.[46] His two chief literary works are *The Complaint of Nature* (*De planctu naturae*) in combined prose and verse, and the *Anticlaudianus,* which we might render *The Rejoinder to Claudian on the Ideal Man. The Complaint* is a dismal affair in which Lady Nature, a figure that owes much to Martianus Capella, complains about the unnatural sexual vices of men. Though distinct, philosophy (represented by Nature) and theology collaborate under God, the ruler of the cosmos. Man is born of Nature, reborn by God's power; but of all her creatures, man alone will not obey her laws.

A far superior poem is the *Anticlaudianus, The Rejoinder to Claudian* in nine books. In Claudian's poem *In Rufinum,* Theodosius' minister Rufinus is painted as the archfiend, the incarnation of human wickedness, entrusted with the destruction of the world. Alan, however, in his poem writes an allegorical epic on the creation of an ideal man, the perfect embodiment of the divine Idea. In a garden of perpetual spring, Lady Nature summons her divine sisters, the virtues (personifications of Paul's fruits of the Spirit, reminiscent of Hermas), to plan the creation of the perfect man, the ideal composite of the divine and human. After long discussion, Phronesis or Wisdom (Aristotle's ethical insight) is delegated to drive to the court of heaven. The chariot is made up of the Trivium and Quadrivium of the mediaeval university; it is drawn by the five Senses, and in it Wisdom is accompanied by Reason and Prudence. The reach the throne of Theology, who directs them, Wisdom must now leave her chariot together with Reason and mount through the vaults of heaven. Here she sees a mystic vision of the blessed, much as one would imagine them from the canvasses of Van Eyck or Fra Angelico. She pauses

[46] On Alan of Lille, see Manitius, *op. cit.,* pp. 794 *ff.;* Raby, *A History of Christian-Latin Poetry,* pp. 297 *ff.;* Curtius, *op. cit.,* pp. 117–22, and *passim; cf.* also Raby, *A History of Secular Latin Poetry,* II. 15 *ff.* For his philosophic and theological doctrine, see Gilson, *History of Christian Philosophy,* pp. 172–78.

at the loveliness of the Virgin; and here Alan devotes a long section to a catalogue of her titles drawn from the Marian tradition: star of the sea, bridal bower, garden enclosed and fountain sealed up, olive, cedar, Eden, wine-cellar, nectar of paradise. When Wisdom finally arrives at the seat of the triune Godhead, surrounded by brilliant springs, the eternal ideas, and the causes of things, her request on behalf of Nature is granted. God bids Nous form the Idea of the perfect soul and Wisdom descends through the heavenly spheres to bring it back to earth. For it Nature fashions a perfect body; the sister virtues contribute their gifts. But soon the cosmic forces of evil rise in revolt, and the poem ends in a *psychomachia* that recalls the *Fight Over Man's Soul* of Prudentius. But Iuvenis (Youth), the newly-created, conquers with the help of the virtues, and the world is transformed into a new Eden ruled by love and harmony, outwardly symbolized by the luxurious blossoming of the gardens and fields.

From the philosophical point of view the poem of Alan is a fascinating fusion of mediaeval Platonism and Aristotelianism; and taken together with the less successful *Complaint of Nature* it is clear that the speculative *doctor universalis* was seriously committed to the problem of moral reform. The *Anticlaudianus*, for all its grandeur, is often a tiresome piece of work. But despite the blatant didacticism, the poet's fertile inventiveness and narrative style keep the allegory moving. It is on the whole a striking imaginative conception which must surely have been known by Dante when he wrote the *Commedia*.

Three monastic poets herald the rise of the more devotional aspect of mediaeval poetic symbolism: Peter Damiani, Bernard of Clairvaux, and Bernard of Cluny or Morlas. After these we shall discuss the growth of Franciscan poetry under the aegis of St. Francis himself, and the Seraphic Doctor, St. Bonaventure. One of the sternest reforming Popes of the Middle Ages, the monk Hildebrand, known as Gregory VII, found a fiery instrument of his designs in the hermit of Ravenna, Peter Damiani (1007–1072).[47] Peter had studied, it is said, at Ravenna, Faenza, and Parma; and, before his ascetical conversion, he opened a school

[47] On Peter Damiani, see Manitius, *op. cit.*, pp. 68 *ff.;* Cross, *op. cit.*, pp. 1053 *f.* with the latest bibliography.

of arts at Ravenna. After some years of holy retirement at Fonte Avellana, Pope Stephen X forced him to come forth in 1057 as Cardinal Bishop of Ostia, and the assumption of this office marked the beginning of those emotional denunciations which made him notorious throughout Italy. Despite his humanistic background, he now preached the terrors of hell-fire, and the need of preparation for death by self-scourging, fasting, and other forms of penance. As Cardinal Bishop and papal legate his influence was great with the popes and clergy of his day, and yet he does not hesitate to castigate the vices of Rome; some of his most vicious epigams survive, as for example:

Vivere vis Romae? clara depromite voce:
plus domino papae quam domno pareo papae.

If at Rome you'd choose to stay,
Then loudly proclaim this word:
'Tis not the Lord Pope that I obey
So much as the pontiff's Lord.

A saintly, though somewhat morbid and unbalanced ascetic, the violence of his imagination is well reflected in *The Book of Gomorrha,* a vivid denunciation of contemporary vice. By way of apology for his indictment, he says (*Liber* § 25):

> Like the innocent Joseph, I should rather be cast into a cistern for accusing my brothers of unnatural vice rather than like the conniving Heli be punished by the Almighty.

Secular learning completely nauseates him: "My grammar is Christ," he writes to a friend (*Epist.* 8.8). We can study, if we will, his austere doctrine in the treatises *Against Intemperate Clerics,* and *On the Monk's Perfection.* But it was inevitable that his imagination would spill over into verse; typical are *The Pains of Hell Fire,* and *Song of a Penitent Monk.* His works stand as a literary monstrosity, a far more vicious indictment of fallen human nature than anything the Romans ever wrote. His morbid mind and fierce darkling terror produced at times exceptional verse. But the emotion is excessive, the horror unrelieved. The vision of the final judgment obsessed his mind; he pictures the sinner struck with terror at the sound of the final trumpet: his tongue grows stiff, his eyes roll, he sweats like a man in a convulsion of sheer fright. This is the heart of *The Day of Death:*

> Day of death, you strike me with dread fear,
> My heart is heavy, my reins dissolve, and all
> My stomach trembles in pain, as my anxious mind
> Depicts the awful horror of my death.
>
> For who could clearly paint that dreadful hour,
> When, life's circuit over, the soul in haste
> Will free itself from the bonds of the sick flesh?
>
> Senses dim, tongue hardens, eyes roll;
> The breast heaves, the throat rasps hoarsely;
> Limbs stiffen, face grows pale—all beauty gone! . . .

And there is much more. The poet himself seems as though seized by some strange catalepsy as he contemplates the passing of his "sick flesh."

Despite the change of style, there has also been attributed to Peter Damiani an elusively delicate paraphrase of the *Song of Songs* which begins:

> Who is this that knocks at my door
> Breaking the dreams of night?
> It is He Who calls:
> Loveliest of virgins, my sister,
> My spouse, my radiant jewel;
> Open quickly, arise, my love.

The Spouse identifies Himself as the Son of the King, come to liberate mankind; the bride replies:

> Straightway then I left my bed
> And ran to raise the latch
> That all my house might open to my Love,
> That my soul might wholly see
> The One it yearns for.

But when the door is opened there is no one there. The bride runs out into the night, and the song concludes:

> The city watchmen found me
> And despoiled me;

They took my shift and gave it back again;
A new song they sang me,
To lead me to the palace of the King.

It is a rudimentary form of verse of quiet passion, which derives its rhythms from the very Latin of Jerome's Vulgate.[48] Whether it came from the same kind that produced the *Day of Death,* we cannot be sure.

The spirit of this haunting paraphrase is perhaps closer to the *Sermons on the Song of Songs* of St. Bernard of Clairvaux. Full of spiritual energy and a zeal that was the fruit of mysticism, Bernard was not only the focal point of the Cistercian movement, but perhaps the most influential monk of the century. As a theologian he scored the rationalist excesses of the French masters, such as Peter Abelard and Gilbert de la Porrée; yet his spirit came to rest in a tender devotion to the humanity of the Savior, which was an anticipation of later Franciscan spirituality. As a poet, however, judging from those of the extant pieces that have any claim to authenticity, we can only consider him mediocre. Thus it is felt by scholars that the famous Rosy Sequence on the Name of Jesus, *Dulcis Iesu Memoria,* though Cistercian in inspiration, is surely not from Bernard's hand.[49]

Like the *Stabat Mater* it is an intensely emotional religious

[48] For the poem see the remarks of Raby, *A History of Christian-Latin Poetry,* pp. 254 *f.* The motif was apparently very common throughout the Middle Ages. In the Latin play *Paphnutius* by the nun Hroswitha of Gandersheim (tenth century), the monk Paphnutius attempts to convert the courtesan Thais by adapting the dialogue of the *Song of Songs.* Scene III begins:

Paphnutius: Thais! Thais!
Thais: Who's there? I do not recognize the voice.
Paphnutius: Thais, it is your lover. Thais!
Thais: Stranger, who are you?
Paphnutius: Arise, my love, my beautiful one, and come!
Thais: But who are you?
Paphnutius: One who loves you.

Indeed, the entire play, for all its faults, is a dramatization of the mediaeval concept of sin and repentance. See the edition by K. Strecker, *Hrotsvithae Opera* (Leipzig, 1930), and the brief note with bibliography in Cross, *op. cit.,* pp. 660–61.

[49] See Cross, *op. cit., s.v.* "Rosy Sequence," pp. 1184 *f.,* and "Jesu, Dulcis Memoria," p. 722.

document: a personal mystical encounter between the soul and God. But the theme is perhaps too long drawn out for modern tastes. Verses 1–3 are a promising, vivid prelude: the poet can think or sing or hear of nothing sweeter than the sacred Name. Several other stanzas develop the theme of seeking, of probing the dark mystery of the divinity. Finally the monk's longing is satisfied, but all too briefly, in a loving union with the Savior; and the tone recalls the *Song of Songs.* In the central portion the poem lacks unity of focus and seems to wander. Finally, with the last strophes, there is the suggestion of a triumphal entry of the King into heaven, and the pious author begs that he may accompany his Lord into Paradise. Despite its defects, the hymn has a directness and intensity that save it from mediocrity.

The Franciscan movement brought a new development in Christian thinking, with consequent effects on the symbolic imagination. It is for us almost unbelievable that the son of the simple Umbrian laborer, Pietro Bernadone, should have inaugurated so profound a revolution. Giovanni, nicknamed Francesco, "the Frenchman," was the first Christian saint to have experienced the stigmata, the physical impression of the wounds of the Crucified; and the Franciscian monks and nuns encouraged a very human devotion to the Passion and wounds of Jesus, and to the sorrows of his afflicted Mother. They were, it seems, the first to encourage the sculptured representations of the Cave at Bethlehem; and it is to their influence that we can trace the spread of the so-called Way of the Cross—representations of the various "stations" or stops on the Via Dolorosa in Jerusalem—that Christians who could not make a pilgrimage to the Holy Land might be able to visit the places in spirit where the precious Blood of the Savior had fallen. Above all, it is important to understand how these devotions, to the Cross and Passion, to the humanity of Jesus and to the sorrows of his Mother, profoundly influenced the poetry of the thirteenth and fourteenth centuries.

The Franciscan poetic tradition can be said to begin with the prose rhythm, written originally in Italian and later translated into Latin, the *Hymn to the Sun* or *Cantico delle creature.*[50] The

[50] See Cross, *op. cit., s.v.* "Canticle of the Sun, The," p. 233, with the references. On the growth of Franciscan spirituality, see Raby, *A History of Christian-Latin Poetry,* pp. 415 *ff.*

Italian is, with good probability, attributed to the hand of St. Francis himself (1186–1226). In form, it is an imitation of the *Laudate*-psalms of the Hebrew psalter, especially the 135th, in which the psalmist calls upon all creation to sing the praise of Iahweh enthroned in His temple in Jerusalem. Francis' *laude* is also indebted to the so-called canticle of the three youths, Sidrach, Misach, and Abdenage, who were allegedly thrust into a fiery oven by the Babylonian king, according to the story in the Book of Daniel (3.52–88). Earlier Christian poets had attempted the subject before, like Walafrid Strabo in his lovely hymn in classic adonics, *The Song of the Three Youths in the Fiery Furnace.* The Italian lines of Francis' poem vary in length and in rhythm, and occasionally rhyme. In their primitive beauty they express Francis' doctrine of the brotherhood of all creatures under the fatherhood of God, the common theme of all Francis' teaching, as we learn from the *Fioretti* or *Little Flowers of St. Francis,* as well as from the life of Francis preserved in Bishop Giacopo of Genua, otherwise known as Iacobus de Voragine (1230–1298).

Just as the 135th psalm calls upon the sun and moon and stars to bless the Lord, so Francis calls upon Brother Sun, sending forth rays as a symbol (*simbolo*) of the Godhead. His brothers are the moon, stars, winds, fire, and terrestrial phenomena; his sisters are the nourishing Mother Earth, and finally Death. A mother produces life, and a sister receives back into the womb of earth all mankind. The poem closes with a prayer (perhaps added within the last months of his life) that all the just may persevere till the end and be not overtaken by Second Death, eternal damnation.

The Latin version is quite good, in the Vulgate tradition, without the charming assonance and rhyme of the Italian. Though far from being great poetry, it is nonetheless a great Christian document; and there breathes throughout the deep, inspired affection for all things created:

O good omnipotent Lord most high
To Thee be all praise, glory, honor and benediction.
To Thee alone do they belong,
And no man is worthy to invoke Thy name.

Praised be my Lord God in all Thy creatures:
First of all in our esteemed brother Sun,
Who makes our day and brings us light,
Lovely is he, radiant and splendid,
A symbol of Thy Godhead.

Praised be my Lord God in my sister Moon
And in all the stars, for the sharp and lovely light
That He has made in them.

Praised be my Lord God in brother Wind,
And in air, and clouds, and all the seasons
Through which He gives nourishment to all His creation.

Praised be my Lord God in sister Water,
For she is so useful, humble, precious, chaste.

Praised be my Lord God in brother Fire,
By whom He brings light in darkness,
Ruddy, flashing, invincible, fierce.

Praised be my Lord God for our Mother Earth;
It is she who supports and feeds us,
Producing abundant fruit
And multicolored buds and herbs.

To Thee be praise, my Lord, for all those
Who for Thy love condone offences,
Who bear trial and illness in patience.
Blessed are they who have borne their lives in peace,
For they shall be crowned by the Most High.

To Thee be praise, my Lord, for our sister Death.
Her no living being can escape.
Woe to those who die in deadly sin.
And blessed are they who, at the hour of death,
Find their hearts in harmony with Thy Will.
For they will never die a second death.

Praise and bless the Lord, all ye creatures,
Serve Him, please Him, in all humility.

The tenderness of Francis' hymn recalls the spirit of Paulinus, Venantius, and Gottschalk. Whether or not this is great poetry it is, in any case, authentic Christianity, expressed within the imaginative terms of Hebrew psalmody. The scholar of Greek philosophy might detect overtones of the Stoic Zeno's doctrine of human brotherhood—but poor Francesco never read Greek. It is a moving piece of mediaeval hymnody, and the doctrine of the unity of all creatures, here expressed in such an earthly, charming way, will later be developed by the Franciscan philosopher Duns Scotus with characteristic subtlety, especially in his symbol of the Tree of material creation.

One of the greatest thinkers of the thirteenth century was John of Fidanza, who entered the Franciscan Order and is known to all as Bonaventure (1221–1274), the Seraphic Doctor, philosopher, and biographer of Francis of Assisi.[51] Whether or not the various poems attributed to him are authentic, they remain true reflections of the Franciscan devotion that was associated with his name. The best known of these is the *Laudismus de Sancta Cruce* which begins *Recordare sanctae crucis,* "Be mindful of the holy Cross." The hymn is a *summa theologiae* of the spirituality of the Cross addressed to the monk, the *Christianus* and *bonus frater* of the text. The imagery ranges through three levels: the Cross as an emblem of the Passion, the Cross as a sacred wood, and the Cross as the epitome of Christ's doctrine, life and death. For the monk, the Cross should be everywhere before him; he should seek it always, eating, drinking, sleeping. The poet then lists the various titles that have been used of the Cross: it is a raft of salvation, a harbor, garden, door, medicine, armor, a charm, a tree of life bearing fruit. Finally, in the spirit of the *Stabat Mater,* the monk asks for the pains of Christ, to be wounded with Him, to embrace Him, to become strong as pain falls on him as a dew. It is fascinating to see how far the Franciscan mysticism has developed the symbols first found in Venantius Fortunatus' hymns to the Holy Rood.

Another superior poet in the tradition of St. Francis was John Pecham, an Englishman who studied at Lewes Priory and at Oxford before entering the Order.[52] He sat at the feet of Bona-

[51] On Bonaventure, see E. Gilson, *The Philosophy of St. Bonaventure* (London, 1938); Cross, *op. cit.*, p. 184, with bibliography. See also Gilson, *History of Christian Philosophy*, pp. 331 *ff.*

[52] On Archbishop John Pecham, see Raby, *A History of Christian-Latin Poetry*, pp. 425 *ff.*; Cross, *op. cit.*, p. 1038. See also Gilson, *History of Christian Philosophy*, pp. 359 *f.*, with the notes.

venture, then returned to Oxford as a lector; in 1275 he was elected Provincial of the English Franciscans; and from 1279 until his death in 1292 he filled the chair of Archbishop of Canterbury, though much against his will. Of all his extant poetry the most strangely moving is the *Philomena*, an allegorical lyric on the nightingale as the Christian soul. It is a most complex conception, but rises to heights of beauty unequalled by any other mediaeval allegory. The poet begins by explaining the various levels of meaning in the nightingale's mystical day. It is to be her last on earth, and flying to a treetop at dawn she begins to pour out her sweet song. Through the hours of Prime and Tierce (in the monastic horarium) the passion of her song swells to great beauty; but at the hour of Sext, or noon, she sinks and falls with the pathetic cry *oci, oci,* and at None, or three o'clock, she dies.

As the poet explains, the nightingale is the soul of man in love with God. But the monastic hours of the nightingale's life represent the history of man on earth in the divine dispensation. At dawn was man's creation, Prime was the hour of the Incarnation, Tierce the time of Christ's life and teaching, Noon the hour of the Passion, Nones the time of his death, Vespers his burial. So, guided by the mystic poet, the monk follows the progress of the soul as it relives the history of salvation. The meditations on Christ's life are episodes of great Franciscan beauty; finally, as the hour of Nones approaches, the poet now, like the nightingale, dies in an ecstasy of union with the Passion of Jesus. In the poignant notes of the nightingale one can almost detect the inspiration of Paulinus and Prudentius; but the full-bodied mysticism owes much to the spirit of St. Francis and Citeaux.

The mediaeval philosophers are not the usual place one would expect to find poetic imagery and symbolism, and yet especially in Duns Scotus (*c.* 1270–1308) and Thomas Aquinas (1226–1274) we find a world that is teeming with life and activity beneath the apparently dry exterior of scholasticism.[53] In the

[53] See on Scotus, Gilson, *History of Christian Philosophy*, pp. 454–64, with the notes; Leff, *Medieval Thought*, pp. 262–72.

On St. Thomas, see Gilson, *The Christian Philosophy of St. Thomas* (New York, 1956); and for the imaginative imagery in Thomas, see especially M. D. Chenu, *Introduction à l'étude de Saint Thomas*

De rerum principio, a treatise almost certainly from the hand of Scotus on the unity of all creatures, we find a remarkably visual exposition of the Scotistic doctrine of matter and form. Scotus was opposed to the Thomistic theory on the nature of Matter; for the Franciscan, all created things, even angelic beings, were composed of a fundamental stuff which he called matter. He thus realizes a more concrete unity among all creatures as they emanate by God's creative activity in the universe. The entire world, he tells us, in an image reminiscent of the mediaeval Paradise-tree, is like a gigantic tree planted and watered by God. It is divided into two main sections or branches, the spiritual and material orders of creation; the flowers stand for the souls of men, and the fruit the hierarchies of angels; the falling leaves are the various accidents, spiritual and material, that subsist in the substances of the world. The image is a remarkable one, not least of all because it might perhaps more conveniently suit the tendencies of modern philosophy and avoid the difficulties inherent in the Thomistic theory of the union between soul and body.

There are no such images in the works of Aquinas; and yet the concrete examples or analogies that lurk behind many of his most abstract discussions suggest an imagination very much alive. Perhaps his most frequent analogies are taken from the operation of the four elements: the action of fire on wood, the flow of water and its reflection of images, the rarity of the atmosphere, and the parting of the sun's rays over the world, with the irridescence of light and color. In discussing causality he reveals his interest in the arts and crafts, in the hammers and axes of the mediaeval carpenter, in the painter's colors, and the statuary of the sculptor in bronze and clay. He is curious about the movement of the heavenly bodies, the attraction of the magnet, the shapes of people's noses and faces, the cleaning and dying of garments and the removal of deep stains, the process of digestion and nutrition, the growth and development of embryos, animals, and men. His

---

d'Aquin (Paris and Montreal, 1950), pp. 145 *ff*. On the poetry, see Raby, *A History of Christian-Latin Poetry*, pp. 402–414; *cf*. also the article "Adoro Te Devote," in Cross, *op. cit.*, p. 19, with a bibliography on the controversy.

mind was ever searching the world for illustrations, analogies, sources of argumentation. When we consider the wide interests reflected in the *Summa* alone, we are more prepared to accept the supreme imaginative transformation that we find in the Eucharistic poems composed for the Office and the Liturgy of Corpus Christi.[54]

In the years 1261–64, Thomas Aquinas had been residing at the papal court of Urban IV, by whom he had been invited to discuss philosophy and theology. Born of noble Italian blood, and a former disciple of Albert the Great, Thomas received his doctorate at Paris in 1257, on the same day as Bonaventure. A brilliant and energetic student, he began early to lecture at Paris on Boethius, and he was soon to become, within the maelstrom of the mid-thirteenth century, the most prominent philosopher of the Church. It was during his stay with Urban IV, according to tradition, that he began his intense study of Aristotle, chiefly through the versions of his fellow Dominican, William of Moerbeke. Urban IV then commissioned Thomas in 1264 to compose the liturgical office of the new feast of Corpus Christi, to be proclaimed to the universal Church on Sept. 8, 1264. It is to Urban's inspiration, therefore, that we owe some of the finest poetry of the Church; indeed, through it, we gain an insight into the imagination of the Angelic Doctor such as we could never have obtained from his theology.

The hymns that Thomas then composed are striking examples of the fusion between theology and the imagination. And yet the feast itself had a popular origin. Some years before, Urban IV had been archdeacon at Liège when Juliana, the saintly nun of Mont Cornillon (*d.* 1258), had a vision of a large moon (or sacramental wafer) within which was a dark flaw: it was interpreted to mean that the liturgy was incomplete without a feast in honor of the sacramental Body of Christ. The feast was celebrated at Liège, and enthusiasm slowly grew. Finally, in 1263, while Urban was Pope, a skeptical priest of Bolsena was said to have seen drops of blood appearing on the consecrated host. It was then

[54] On the institution of the Feast of Corpus Christi, see F. Oppenheim, in *Enciclopedia cattolica italiana* (Vatican City, 1946–57), III. 611–13.

that Urban decided to act. Thomas may well have adapted an already existing Cistercian Office composed by John of Mont Cornillon; some have even doubted whether our extant texts are a precise copy of the hymns that came from Thomas's hand; but in the present state of scholarship we can do no more than accept them.

At any rate, we have today three hymns, for Vespers (*Pange, lingua*), Matins (*Sacris sollemniis*), and Lauds (*Verbum supernum*), and a Sequence for the Mass (*Lauda, Sion*); as for the *Adoro te, devote,* we are not certain that it is by Thomas. What is so remarkable is the variety of approach, in each of these hymns, to the same subject. The Vespers hymn, *Pange, lingua* begins with a paraphrase of Venantius' hymn to the Cross; its central note is the origin of the sacramental mystery in the humanity of Christ, and it paints a charming picture of his sitting down to eat with his friends. The hymn at Matins, *Sacris sollemniis,* is written in classic Asclepiads in imitation of an inferior hymn by Rhaban Maurus. The pagan classical rhythm seems at once to strike a more joyous note; and the poem itself is a hymn of glory on the hieratic aspect of the Eucharistic as a sacrificial act, as a ceremonial entrusted to the Church's special ministers. From this point of view the tone of the piece was most probably suggested by the doctrine of the Pauline epistle to the Hebrews. The last two strophes stress the link between the Eucharist and Old Testament typology; but the lines beginning *Panis angelicus* far transcend any cold didacticism. We are familiar with the Latin words from the many musical settings of modern composers:

Panis angelicus fit panis hominum
dat panis caelicus figuris terminum.
O res mirabilis: manducat Dominum
pauper, servus et humilis.

The final doxology is absorbed into the vision:

Te, trina Deitas unaque, poscimus,
sic nos tu visita, sicut te colimus:
per tuas semitas duc nos quo tendimus,
ad lucem quam inhabitas.

Pauline, Platonic, and mediaeval imagery blend into one. The bread of angels, now consumed by the poor, has here a mystic Grail-like quality, drawing all mankind to the place where God dwells in a region of light. All men's ideals, all man's quest for glory, are summed up in the vision of the mysterious Bread, recalling perhaps the revelation made to the saintly Juliana.

The hymn for Lauds, *Verbum supernum prodiens,* is partly based on an Advent hymn in the Ambrosian manner found in manuscripts of the tenth century. It contains one fine phrase, *in vitae ferculo* (line 7), "on the (dinner) course of life"; but it hardly initiates the theme of the Eucharistic institution when it abruptly ends. Unless our text has been badly abridged, this would seem to be the poorest by far of all the collection.

The sequence for the Mass, *Lauda, Sion,* resembles in style some of the hymns of Adam of St. Victor; it is unique in the way the bones of dogmatic controversy on the Eucharist are covered with the flesh of a rapidly moving, vivid poetry. Poetically and theologically, it is the climax of all the hymns recited at the canonical hours. At the same time, it chiefly celebrates the mystery by which the sacred appearances are multiplied despite the unity of the Body of Christ. It is an aspect that had not been treated in the other hymns, and it is very aptly kept for the actual performance of the Mass liturgy.

The sequence, like so many other mediaeval poems, has three levels corresponding to the Origenist division of world history: Shadow, Image, and Reality. The Shadow is contained in all the Old Testament types: Sion for the body of the faithful, the passover celebrating the crossing of the Red Sea, the paschal lamb, the sacrifice of Isaac. The Image is the period of the Church on earth, during which the mysteries are celebrated in symbols. Here the wonder of the Eucharistic multiplication is stressed, and the unity of the body of the faithful in the unique Body of Christ. All men, regardless of wealth, color, or status, can approach the sacred table. Finally, the sequence ends with a communal prayer in which the faithful pray to be admitted to the Reality, the banquet table of the Risen Shepherd in heaven. The technical and metrical precision of the poem together with its marvelous sweep make it one of the classics of mediaeval poetry. Its didacticism is never repellent or excessive—just like the instructive, narrative windows in the cathedral of Chartres. Like them, the *Lauda, Sion* has a vitality and vigor which could only come from the deep sincerity of Christian conviction.

The short hymn, *Adoro te devote,* is another tiny jewel of mediaeval Eucharistic devotion. Found in two fourteenth century manuscripts, one from Assisi, and another from Monte Cassino, it seems never to have got into an Office and was used instead for private devotion. The attribution to Thomas is unfortunately not quite secure. The poem develops from the opening statement of the mystery, the *latens deitas,* the "hidden Godhead," suggestive of the entire mystery of the universe. It is a poem which recalls the Augustinian doctrine of signs and symbols in the *De doctrina christiana* of which we shall have more to say farther on: signs lead men to the truth of created things, and things lead men to God. It is this doctrine, here so intimately linked with the mystery of the Sacrament, that will be focal for our final solution. Its beauty evades translation:

Adoro te devote, latens deitas
quae sub his figuris vere latitas;
tibi se cor meum totum subicit,
quia te contemplans totum deficit. . . .

Pie pelicane, Iesu domine,
me immundum munda tuo sanguine;
cuius una stilla salvum facere
totum mundum posses omni scelere.

The doxological strophe resumes the symbol of the veil:

Iesu quem velatum nunc aspicio,
quando fiet illud, quod tam sitio?
ut te revelata cernens facie
visu sim beatus tuae gloriae.

Here the Shadow-Image-Reality theme is expressed in the veil-symbol. The Eucharist now becomes a touchstone of faith, as well as the central Cipher which will lead us to ultimate Truth. Beginning with the notion of the Sacrament as a memorial of the Supper, the poet develops the moral implication which the Christian must draw: the living in Christ. Once again past and present are united. Then, after an address to Jesus, the divine Pelican nursing his offspring on his own blood, the poet turns to the symbol of the veil that shrouds and hides the Godhead, and closes with a longing to see the Reality. The deep sentiment of the hymn suggests that it is rather to be associated with the Cistercian or Franciscan movement and that it is not from the hand of Thomas at all.

For our final piece we could choose none better than the *Dies Irae,* attributed to the Franciscan Thomas of Celano (d. about 1260), perhaps the most perfect mediaeval poem of its kind.[55] Based on the ominous words of the prophet Zephaniah predicting the wrathful coming of Iahweh, which the Roman liturgy adapted for the *Blessing over the Grave* of the burial service, the hymn is the culmination of a number of earlier attempts to portray the Last Judgment. But though the tradition is a long one, going back to Commodian's primitive acrostic on the Last Day (about A.D. 250), the *Dies Irae* marks the end of possible development. There are overtones of Paul's description of the Final Coming to the Thessalonians; but we are perhaps to imagine the scene as it was carved over the gates of cathedrals like Notre Dame and Chartres. The poem itself is not liturgical, but rather a very personal meditation in the Franciscan manner. As the monk thinks of the Last Day, and how perhaps it might overtake him in his lifetime, he is filled with terror. The solemn Judge takes His seat as did the mediaeval magistrates presiding over a capital crime:

Iudex ergo cum censebit,
quidquid latet, apparebit:
nil inultum remanebit.
quid sum miser tunc dicturus,
quem patronum rogaturus,
dum vix iustus sit securus?

And again:

[55] On Thomas of Celano there has been a good deal of controversy in modern times, not only about the authenticity of the *Dies Irae* but also on the historicity of his two lives of St. Francis of Assisi. See the bibliography in Cross, *op. cit.*, p. 1354. For a good analysis of the *Dies Irae* and a discussion of its original text, see Raby, *A History of Christian-Latin Poetry*, pp. 443-50, with the bibliography, p. 485.

Iuste iudex ultionis,
donum fac remissionis
ante diem rationis.

The language here is legal: the poet is summoned before the Judge on the *dies rationis.* In accord with the imperial Code the just judge, the *iustus iudex,* must find either for (*ultio*) or against (*remissio*) the accused on the evidence brought forward, either in oral testimony or in a *libellus accusatorius,* a written denunciation. But the poet suddenly feels abandoned: he can find no *patronus,* no lawyer or advocate to plead his innocence. He feels his guilt, and appeals to the silent magistrate for mercy instead of rigorous justice. His appeal now becomes rhetorical: he reminds the Lord of his own wanderings through Palestine in search of the lost sheep, of his kindness to the Magdalen and the Good Thief. As the division is made between sheep and goats, and as the eternal fires crackle, the poet makes his final impassioned plea. But the vision fades, the poet is still alive on earth, and he prays for a sense of humility and contrition

A heart crushed as ashes—

as the dust of penance with which he might befoul his head, or like the ashes and dust to which all mortal bodies return. At the end, he begs the Lord to watch over the last days of his life:

Gere causam mei finis.

The last six lines, in which there is a prayer for the departed, has been added by the Church as early as the fourteenth century in order to adapt the poem to the immediate context of the funeral liturgy. But the change in metre and rhyme-scheme shows that the lines are not authentic.

Apart from the vast influence the *Dies Irae,* with its plain-chant melody, has exercised on the imaginations of so many Christian poets and artists, it stands as a monumental symbol of the ideal Christian poem according to the doctrine of Paulinus of Nola. Hebrew, Christian, and even secular symbols are fused in the poetic structure to express the poet's anxiety and the decision to which he has come on the problem of his sinful, guilt-ridden condition. No Christian poem has better suggested the Christian's inner torment set against the eschatological view of history: it is the crisis of both the Christian and the Church, set between two divine theophanies, Christ's life and death on earth and his Final Coming. On this note it re-echoes the voice of Zephaniah: the day of Iahweh has indeed come, and men must work out their salvation through fear and trembling, dwelling in a valley of death. It is ironic that the greatest poem of the Middle Ages should be a trumpet call of doom, the Judgment, and the passing of all creation,

tuba mirum spargens sonum
per sepulchra regionum
coget omnes ante thronum.

Yet it is not without that touch of human hope that has ever given men courage to live:

qui Mariam absolvisti,
et latronem exaudisti,
mihi quoque spem dedisti.

It is as though all men were brigands, all women adulteresses—but all are redeemed. The poet's stark message is, in the end, one with the evangelical *kerygma.*

The Solution of the Christian Dilemma

CHAPTER ELEVEN

IT HAS been the purpose of these chapters to explore some of the vast areas of the Christian imagination down to the Middle Ages and to attempt to document the view that Christianity created a remarkable tension deep in man's soul. It was indeed a unique phenomenon of the primitive Church that the earliest writers experienced a strong compulsion to reject the works of the imagination, to abandon poetry as a medium of expression. The writings of Plato and Plotinus had encouraged a deep distrust of the fantasy as the source of all error; and poetry and drama in general do not flourish in any Platonic atmosphere, since it is rather the disembodied Idea and not the concrete experience that is for the Platonist the source of truth. Christianity also drew from Stoicism, and this is reflected especially in the attitude of some of the early Fathers towards the passions, and in the dream of an ascetic apathy which could be in some measure attainable on earth.[56] What is strange is that the early Christian view of poetry cannot be squared with the study of the Old Testament: the psalms, the prophets, the Song of Songs—so much of Hebrew

[56] For the early period see Michel Spanneut, *Le stoïcisme des Pères de l'Eglise de Clément de Rome à Clément d'Alexandrie* (Paris, 1957), with the very complete bibliography, pp. 435 *ff*. For the important influence of Stoic ideas of mixture during the patristic controversies on the Incarnation, see H. A. Wolfson, *The Philosophy of the Church Fathers*. Volume I. *Faith, Trinity, Incarnation* (Cambridge, Mass., 1956), pp. 379–84.

literature was sheer poetry and imaginative prose. And yet, even in the mild Paulinus we read:

> Hearts pledged to Christ are closed to Apollo,
> And deny entrance to the goddesses of song.

This turning from the harmless pleasure (as Aristotle called it) of music and song, this revulsion and rejection of the world, was preached by the early writers and founded on the eschatological vision of Paul and of Jesus Himself. Psychologically speaking, the early Christians felt that the deepest demands of faith could only be satisfied by a definitive rejection of the world, by death, either real or symbolic, by martyrdom or the daily dying of asceticism. This attitude seems to extend itself to all of secular studies and occupations. Indeed, Jerome's famous vision of the Judgment Seat, however we are to understand it, is not untypical.[57]

Jerome's story is related in a letter he wrote to the lady Eustochium, for whom he acted as spiritual guide. On a journey to the East about the year 374, Jerome caught a fever and was close to death. During his delirium, he later wrote, he thought he had a vision in which he found himself before the Judgment Seat of Christ; accused and convicted of reading the pagan authors, he tells Eustochium, he was scourged until he begged for mercy and promised to give up his beloved classics. Later, when he recovered, Jerome does not assert that he gave up his favorite authors, but that from then on he read the Scriptures with as much care as he had given to secular works. The delirium-dream,

[57] The account is given in Jerome, *Epistles* 22.30, written most probably in the year 384, almost ten years after the alleged event. There is a convenient text and translation in F. A. Wright, *Select Letters of St. Jerome* (London, 1933), pp. 52 *ff.*; and *cf.* the narrative in Maisie Ward, *Saints Who Made History: The First Centuries* (New York, 1959), pp. 212 *ff.* The problem is shrewdly discussed by Edward A. Quain, "St. Jerome as a Humanist," in *A Monument to Saint Jerome: Essays on Some Aspects of His Life, Works, and Influence*, edited by F. X. Murphy (New York, 1952), pp. 203–32, especially pp. 228 *f.* For a brief bibliography, see Cross, *op. cit.*, pp. 719–20. One should also consult, Gerard L. Ellspermann, *The Attitude of the Early Christian Latin Writers Toward Pagan Literature and Learning* (Catholic University Patristic Studies 82, Washington, 1949), pp. 126 *ff.*

perhaps embellished for the instruction of his spiritual charge, reflects Jerome's feelings of guilt for his attraction to the classical authors, and for his neglect of those who spoke the message of the Lord.

Even Basil experienced a similar dilemma. His great *Address to the Youth,*[58] which seemed at the time such an extraordinary liberating force, still remains grudging in its recognition of the place of the imagination in the training of the Christian. Secular learning is like the leaves which protect the fruit, even as they confer upon the tree a certain grace and beauty. But, in the analysis, it is only because non-Christian learning may somehow be useful, at least in understanding error, that Basil will allow the young Christian, in the famous simile of the bee, to suck the pagan honey. As he says (*Address to the Youth* 4):

> We shall not therefore approve of the poets when . . . they portray men drunk or in love, or when they equate happiness with an abundant table and licentious songs. And least of all should we pay attention to them when they narrate any story about the gods. . . .

Of the prose writers, we must avoid those passages in which they tend to fabricate for the entertainment of their audience:

> But we should use rather those passages in which they praise goodness and condemn vice. The bee, in addition to the fragrance and color of a flower, is able to draw from it honey as well. So too those engaged in literature should be able to store away in their souls not only what is sweet and pleasant but also what is profitable for their

[58] For a text and an English version, see the Loeb edition by R. J. Deferrari, *Saint Basil: the Letters* (4 vols., London, 1926–34), IV. 379 *ff*. The *Address* is really an instruction or conference which Basil wrote for young students—possibly, as some would say, his own nephews—who were under his direction (see § 1). The seminary order probably included the reading of pagan Greek authors in addition to the Scriptures, and Basil's instruction is perhaps designed to meet difficulties or objections raised by the pupils or their teachers against the use of such texts in the monastery. On Basil, see H. von Campenhausen, *The Fathers of the Greek Church* (New York, 1959), pp. 80–94; *cf*. also Cross, *op. cit*., p. 138.

> souls. Thus our attitude towards pagan literature should be that of the bee. For the bee does not approach all flowers indiscriminately, nor does it try to carry off everything that it lights upon. Rather it takes away only so much as is suitable for what it is doing, and leaves the rest untouched. So too we will take from these writings, if we are wise, only what is suitable and has kinship with the truth, and we will pass over the rest.

Basil's view, therefore, is essentially clear and does not, in the long run, differ substantially from the position maintained by the Greek Fathers from the second century:

> When we pluck the blossoms from a rose bush, we avoid the thorns. So too in gathering what is useful from this literature, we must protect ourselves from what is harmful. We must, at the very outset, scrutinize each doctrine and attempt to harmonize it with our purpose.

And this fits in precisely with what he had said to his young seminary charges at the outset (*Address to the Youth* 2):

> We believe that this mortal life of ours has no value in itself, and hence we do not consider anything to be good which contributes to it alone.

Basil's position is basically an adaptation of Plutarch's analogy of the bee-image in his *How to Study Poetry*. The problem for Plutarch and his audience was how to derive profit from passages in the classical authors which were immoral or obscene. Some of the earlier commentators on Homer were wont to turn every line to profit by suggesting an allegorical or moral interpretation. But Plutarch has no patience with the allegorizers. Hence he proposes the analogy of the bee. When the student comes to an objectionable passage, he is not troubled by the content but merely sucks from the passage whatever he can—presumably lessons of style, diction, and the like. But for Basil the analogy works differently. The Christian bee uses all of pagan literature as Plutarch's bee selected from the immoral passages. We remove from such authors, in Basil's view, only such doctrines which are consonant with Christian doctrine or else we learn from them how ephemeral are the non-Christian's pleasures and beliefs. Basil, as a man of wide culture and education, must surely have been more flexible than this in practice. But, if we may presume that his *Address* was a reply to an actual question, to a complaint perhaps against those Christian teachers who used the pagan authors in their curricula, the structure of his cautious reply becomes somewhat more clear. His main intention is to have students read the classic authors with intelligence. In this he is successful, though it must be admitted that his actual criteria are narrow and leave much to be desired.

Basil's friend, Gregory of Nazianzus, preferred to write poetry rather than explore the problems of the Christian imagination. The enormous bulk of verse that he left is proof enough that he thought it valuable. In a piece entitled *On My Poetry* (II.1.39) he attempted to explain the reasons which drew him—as it did Prudentius of Saragossa—to the writing of verse in his old age. As so much of his work, it is colorless and dull; but the four reasons he gives are suggestive and courageously outspoken. In the first place, he explains, he finds the restraint of verse a fine discipline on what he calls his facility, his lack of moderation; secondly, he felt that poetry was an excellent medium for the instruction of the young (and this explains why so much of his verse consists of mnemonics on the Bible and the life of Christ); thirdly, Christians should be able to compete with pagan poets, if not in style, then surely in thought and contemplation; and fourthly, Gregory simply declares that he is, like an old and tired swan, singing a sweet song of farewell to life before he passes on. Gregory's piece, if far from solving the problem of Christian poetry, is a touching and forthright testament, worthy of being read as a poet's expression of the meaning of his craft.

But among the early Fathers it was chiefly Augustine who possessed the most balanced view on the place of literature, music, and the arts in the life of the Christian. In the treatise *On Christian Doctrine* (I.5),[59] he uses the simile of the pilgrim travelling through foreign countries towards his homeland; so too,

[59] In the *Retractations* Augustine explains the structure of this sprawling work as follows (*Retr.* 2.4.30): "The first three books aid in the comprehension of the Scriptures, and the fourth teaches us how to communicate the facts that we have understood." In general, books

> We are wanderers from God on the road of this mortal life; thus, if we wish to return to our native city, we must use (*uti*) this world, and not take pleasure (*frui*) in it. In this way the invisible attributes of God may be clearly seen, being understood through created reality—that is, we will be able to comprehend the eternal and the spiritual through things that are of space and time.

Indeed, this doctrine of the use of creatures in order to understand the mysteries of the universe is further explained in the second book of *On Christian Doctrine* (II.1–6) in Augustine's discussion of signs and symbols. There he teaches that the entire problem of communicating Christian doctrine must be approached with an understanding of signs. Augustine distinguishes signs used in communication by animals, signs of different kinds (natural and conventional) used by men, signs used by Christ on earth, and finally the signs used in the Scriptures by which God communicates to men through men. But signs, Augustine insists, are meant to lead men to *things* (*ibid.* I.2); and things are to lead men ultimately to God. Created things are not strictly *signs;* but Augustine's distinction of use and enjoyment merely serves to emphasize the fact that all of created reality is intended to bring man to God.

Thus it is wrong to assert that Augustine's only interest in the arts and in secular learning was as a help in understanding the Scriptures. And even if certain passages in his works seem to imply this, his own attitude in practice was far less severe. As a

---

I–II discuss the means of arriving at truth through signs and things, and in particular by a study of the sciences and liberal arts. Book III deals with the interpretation of signs as they occur in the Scriptures (what today would be called hermeneutics), concluding with a discussion of the importance of rhetoric as a means of understanding the Bible. Book IV treats mainly of the new Christian rhetoric, the manner of preaching the Gospel of Jesus; but it also dilates a good deal on the use of rhetoric in the Scriptures. There is a good translation, with introduction, by J. J. Gavigan, in the *Fathers of the Church* vol. IV (New York, 1947), pp. 3–235. See especially the discussion by Ralph A. Marcus, "St. Augustine on Signs," *Phronesis* 2(1957), 60–83.

former teacher of rhetoric, he realized the importance of the liberal curriculum for the development of the mind. As he says in the second book of *On Christian Doctrine* (II.18):

> We ought not to neglect literature simply because its patron god is Mercury, any more than we ignore justice and virtue because there are temples to these virtues. . . . Rather, every good and true Christian should be aware that truth is the Lord's no matter where he may find it.

Literature, rhetoric, history, mathematics, philosophy—all these are the "spoils of Egypt" which the new Israelites take with them in their quest for the Land of Promise. As he says (*ibid.* II.40):

> And wherever the pagan philosophers, especially the Platonists, have said things which are quite truthful and in accordance with Christian belief, we should not be afraid to appropriate them from those who are, in a sense, the unlawful possessors.

This, indeed, was what the Israelites did when they fled from Egypt; and so too the Christian may take with him whatever he needs for his new life. The good things which we find in secular learning, he continues, are like gold and silver, dug "from the mines of divine providence, everywhere present."

From a narrower point of view, Augustine saw that many of the problems raised by the Scriptures and Christian theology could only be solved by a thorough study of human disciplines. Hence the value of mathematics, mineralogy, botany, zoology, and history for the understanding of many passages in the Bible (*ibid.* II.16, 28). Here in the sciences and arts we have the key to many of the obscure symbols and signs of the Old Testament. Indeed, Augustine must have realized that his own facility in the comprehension of the Scriptures came largely from his wide reading and background. Thus even in this area his attitude is far more liberal than, for example, St. Basil's. But in a larger sense, though Christian doctrine is the ultimate norm of truth, for Augustine all truth is Christian: "all truth is the Lord's" no matter where we may discover it. Hence it is that Augustine seems more at ease with literature, the arts, and sciences than any other Father of the Church. He had even planned to write a series of treatises on the liberal arts—his knowledge of mathematics, geometry, and biology was elementary—and we have a reflection of this in his work *On Music* and in the rhetorical sections of *On Christian Doctrine.*

It is clear from his works that he enjoyed literature and poetry. In a letter to his friend, the imperial official Darius (*Epist.* 231),[60] he quotes with approval Horace's theory of the value of literature for the healing of the soul. Horace in his second epistle (*Epist.* I.2) speaks of the "book and lamp" which are a cure for the disturbing passions of the heart; reading is a *pium piaculum,* a "gentle remedy," like the recitation of a magical prayer (*Epist.* I.1.36–7). So too Augustine tells Darius: "By the medicine of the word we may heal, as it were incantation, the serpent's bite." It is Augustine who has introduced into the Horatian quotation the reference to *Genesis;* but there is no rejection of the works of the imagination, no narrowness in his ultimate synthesis. Far deeper than Ambrose or Jerome, Augustine's view was that there were two paths to Truth: one through the signs of the Scriptures, the other through the signs and ciphers of the world of science, philosophy, and art. There is always a hierarchy of values in the quest for God, but never for Augustine a distortion.

This was the synthesis which was channelled to the Middle Ages through the *Divine Institutes* of Cassiodorus, even though it did not everywhere prevail. Cassiodorus, after a successful

[60] *Epist.* 231 to Darius, an official at the court of Valentinian III, was written in the year 429 to accompany copies of Augustine's *Confessions, On Providence,* and several other works. The quotation and comment on Horace occurs at the close of § 3 and beginning of § 4. The lines of Horace quoted are:

> laudis amore tumes? sunt certa piacula, quae te
> ter pure lecto poterunt recreare libello.
>
> Do you swell with love of praise? Then read
> Three times a book whose charms may work
> To cure you.

For a translation, see J. H. Baxter, *St. Augustine: Select Letters* (London, 1930), 452–53. For a discussion of Augustine's theory of literature and poetry, see Bernard F. Huppé, *Doctrine and Poetry: Augustine's Influence on Old English* (State University of New York: 1959), especially pp. 3–24.

career as a civil servant under Theodoric, had tried in vain to establish a theological school at Rome after the model of Alexandria. Thus the blueprint for his monastic curriculum of studies, embodied in his *Divine Institutes,* had a far deeper vision than some modern critics would allow. For, although he borrowed the principle of the primacy of the Scriptures from Alexandria, it was from his "father Augustine," as he affectionately calls him, that Cassiodorus drew his fundamental inspiration. There are two ways to God: the first through the Scriptures; the second through the knowledge of the sciences and arts, rising, as he says, from grammar even to the stars. Thus we know that Cassiodorus expended almost as much effort on the gathering of books dealing with the arts and sciences as he did on the manuscripts—those "corrected codices"—of the Bible and the Fathers. It was through Cassiodorus' vision that war was waged against the devil with pen and ink throughout the numerous Benedictine scriptoria that proliferated on the Continent and in the British Isles.

At the same time, it was long before the haunting figure of Jerome's anxiety-vision could be completely exorcised from the Christian conscience. The opposition to pagan Rome, the withdrawal into the desert to become "martyrs in conscience," the rejection phenomena of conversion—all served to support the extreme eschatological views which dominated the temper of the primitive Church. That poetry could once again charm the mind's pain was shown by Paulinus and Prudentius, by Romanos of Constantinople, by Venantius and Walafrid. The poetic theory of Paulinus of Nola, together with Augustine's more liberal view of human knowledge, especially as it was transmitted by Cassiodorus, slowly cut a swathe through which many later harvesters could follow. But it is clear, as we have seen, that the poetic imagination had already operated in writers like Paul and John, Ignatius of Antioch, Hermas, Methodius, Origen, and many more. And, it should be noted, all these writers drew abundant inspiration from the poetry and prose of the Old Testament. All, to a greater or less extent, used the allegoric mode of interpretation which had entered Christianity through Philo and the Stoics. Thus the power of the imagination continued to hold sway, even in authors who, like Gregory of Nyssa, held that the root of error was in "a certain kind of imagining (*phantasia*) about the truth which occurs in the soul."[61] The rejection of the imagination had, in fact, only created other forms of outlet. For the daring poetic imagery of the Song of Songs, of Pauline ecstasy, and the vision of the Apocalypse continued to exercise a profound influence down to the Middle Ages.

Thus the solution to our problem is at once simple and manifold. The history of Christianity suggests that the imaginative and creative drives cannot long be repressed: they will always emerge and have their way, even in the presence of the Transcendent and with the awareness that the visible structures of this world will pass away. The operation of man's creative imagination is different from what we call reason—but its operation is just as essential. For the Christian, as we have seen, its scope was the tension between Time and Eternity, between the Immanent and the Transcendent, that was the direct result of the biblical message. As Paulinus sang:

> Man is a slender thing, of sickly body
> And passing season, and—without Christ—
> Shadow and dust.

It is clear now that the great Christian writer and artist may incline now to one pole, and now to another; for the two are, in a sense, antithetical. He may sing of the sins of the flesh or the terrors of the Last Day; of the joys of earth or the mystical espousals of Heaven. But he will never destroy the tension which is at the heart of his imaginative creativity. Thus our survey has tried to show how the Christian tradition was fed in different ways from different, and sometimes opposing, sources; and how it grew strong with the intuitive awareness, so beautifully expressed by Augustine, that all truth is the Lord's no matter what the source. Augustine's doctrine of symbols as a clue to the ambiguities of communication, taken with his view of Truth, is the ultimate

[61] Gregory, *The Life of Moses*, ii. 23; see the edition by Jean Daniélou, *Grégoire de Nysse: La Vie de Moïse* (ed. 2, Sources chrétiennes, Paris, 1955), with Introduction, pp. ii *ff*. On Gregory, see H. von Campenhausen, *The Fathers of the Greek Church*, pp. 107–116.

answer to the problem we have been investigating in these pages. The Greek poet Sophocles once said: "Only in old age does man learn wisdom" (*Antigone* 1353). Augustine's Wisdom is man's heaven-sent gift to help him penetrate the signs of the universe and reach the Transcendent. For this, all the world's wisdom, all man's faculties, are requisite. This is the meaning of the divine image that is in man.

Thus the dilemma posed by the problem of the imagination and the process of Christian communication is solved by experience: it is clarified today as it was solved in the past, by the personal struggles of the men who make Christianity what it is, by their deeper vision of the Reality that gives coherence to the things of sense. Man's travail issues forth in further light—as Shadow and Image merge into Truth. But the veil of the Christian mysteries can only be pierced by the thrust of man's creative spirit under the impulse of the divine Love and Wisdom; and here, as always, the imagination must play an integral role. For it is part of the mystery of the universe, as Augustine saw, that the Godhead must somehow hide beneath insubstantial figures.

Index